MICHIGAN
Real Estate Basics

Dearborn™
Real Estate Education

e a great deal of care has been taken to provide accurate and current information, the
, suggestions, general principles, and conclusions presented in this text are subject to
l, state, and federal laws and regulations, court cases, and any revisions of same. The
er is urged to consult legal counsel regarding any points of law. This publication should
be used as a substitute for competent legal advice.

Senior Vice President and General Manager: Roy Lipner
Publisher and Director of Distance Learning: Evan M. Butterfield
Editorial Project Consultant: Marie Spodek, DREI
Development Editor: Amanda Rahn
Acting Editorial Production Manager: Daniel Frey
Typesetter: Janet Schroeder
Creative Director: Lucy Jenkins
Cover and Text Design: Gail Chandler

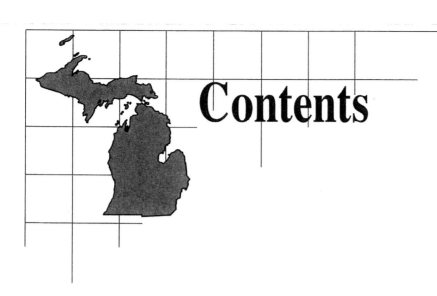

Contents

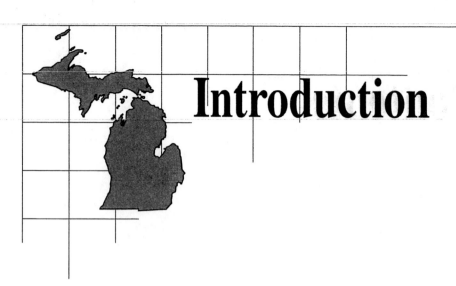

Introduction

Over the last century, all 50 states and the District of Columbia have enacted laws, rules, and regulations to govern the real estate profession. These laws have been enacted to protect the public—buyers, sellers, landlords, and tenants—from dishonest, careless, or unethical practices by real estate licensees. Essentially, the laws provide a framework to ensure that licensees are competent and engage in acceptable business behaviors. Across the United States, some of these laws and regulations are so similar that they can be considered national or generic real estate principles. Many of the important details, however, vary greatly among the states. In order to ensure that you are competent in your profession and that you pass the licensing exam, it's vital that you understand both the big-picture principles *and* the state-specific details.

This book has been primarily designed to supplement a general real estate principles text, and you will find a convenient correlation table that illustrates where the general topics are addressed in a variety of other publications. However, this *Basics* also provides a valuable overview of state law and practice used on its own.

No book writes itself. Like a real estate transaction, this book is the product of teamwork and cooperation among professionals. The following individuals contributed their expertise, industry knowledge, and practical insight to this book:

About the Author

Grace Ronkaitis, JD, is a Michigan attorney, educator, estate broker, licensed residential builder, and a network television director and producer. Grace began her career as a real estate salesperson while she was in college more than two decades ago and has never left the real estate field. She is an active broker participating in property management and commercial brokerage. An accomplished real estate instructor, she is one of the founding partners of **Active Education LLC,** which specializes in real estate continuing education. Grace also practices real estate and business law in order to help others avoid litigation by proper planning, preventative practices, and sound policies.

Content Reviewer

Lori Chmura, Middleton Real Estate Training, Inc.

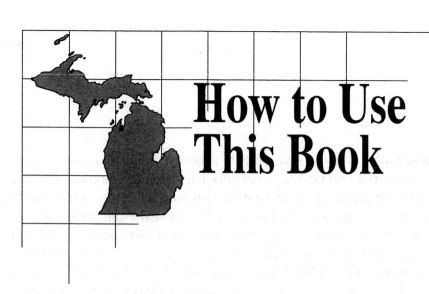

How to Use This Book

The conversion table below provides a quick and easy reference for *Michigan Real Estate Basics* in conjunction with various principles books. For instance, *Michigan Real Estate Basics'* Chapter 2, "Operating a Real Estate Business," may be read in conjunction with Chapters 5 and 20 in *Modern Real Estate Practice;* Chapters 7, 9, and 15 in *Real Estate Fundamentals;* Chapters 13, 14, 16, and 17 in *Mastering Real Estate Principles;* and Lessons 13, 14, and 17 in *SuccessMaster*™ software.

Michigan Real Estate Basics	*Modern Real Estate Practice,* 16th Edition	*Real Estate Fundamentals,* 5th Edition	*Mastering Real Estate Principles,* 3rd Edition	*SuccessMaster*™ (National) Software
1. Licensing Overview	——	——	16	16
2. Operating a Real Estate Business	5, 20	7, 9, 15	13, 14, 16, 17	13, 14, 17
3. Agency Overview	4, 5, 6, 17	9	13, 24	13, 24
4. Contracts And Closings Overview	6, 10, 11, 13, 21, 22	6, 7, 10, 16, 17	3, 10, 11, 12, 14	3, 10, 11, 12, 14
5. License Law Enforcement Overview	4, 5	——	13, 16	13, 16
6. Specialty Topics	8, 16, 18	5, 8, 11	8, 9, 18	8, 9, 18
7. Title Issues	7, 10, 19	3, 10, 14	3, 4, 5	3, 4, 5, 26

Licensing Overview

Real estate practices in Michigan are governed by Public Act 299 of 1980, which is referred to as the *Occupational Code*. This law regulates the licensing of various occupations, including real estate. It also authorizes the Department of Consumer and Industry Services, Bureau of Commercial Services, referred to as the Department, to administer this law. The Occupational Code creates and empowers the Michigan Board of Real Estate Brokers and Salespersons, referred to as the Board, to work jointly under the statute and to assist the Department in adopting a set of administrative rules and regulations to define the statutory law.

The Occupational Code is the law as drafted by the state legislature. The rules are Department policies as to how the Code will be interpreted and enforced. The Board members assist the Department in the implementation of the act. The rules have the same force and effect as the law and provide more detail for the administration of the law and guidelines for the real estate licensee. The law may only be changed by a vote of the legislature. The Department may change the rules and regulations, as required.

This first chapter covers the licensing agency and licensing issues: activities requiring licensure and exemptions, license categories, and licensing requirements and renewals.

A.   BOARD OF REAL ESTATE BROKERS AND SALESPERSONS

1.A.1   What is the name of the Michigan real estate regulatory body?

The regulatory body in Michigan is called the Department of Consumer and Industry Services, Bureau of Commercial Services (Department). The Department's home Web page is http://michigan.gov/cis.

1.A.2   How many members are on the Board? How long may they serve?

The Board of Real Estate Brokers and Salespersons (Board) is under the umbrella of the Department. The Board is made up of nine voting members who must be at least 18 years of age and reside in Michigan. The governor makes the appointments with the advice and consent of the Senate. For representational input, six are Michigan real estate licensees and three are nonlicensees that represent the public. The three public members may not hold a real estate license or be married to a real estate licensee, nor can they have a material financial interest in the business of real estate.

Appointments are for four years unless a person is appointed to fill a vacancy, in which case he or she will serve for the balance of the term. No member is allowed to serve more than two consecutive terms.

1.A.3   Who does the day-to-day work?

The Department consists of a director as its executive head and other employees of the Department of Commerce who perform the day-to-day work. The governor appoints the director with the advice and consent of the Senate.

1.A.4   What are the statutory duties?

Licensing duties are divided between the Department and the Board. The Board interprets licensing requirements, furnishes aid in investigations, determines acceptable practices, and assesses penalties. If a particular duty is not specifically entrusted to the Board, then it will fall on the Department as a whole.

With the advice of the Board, one of the Department's primary duties is to issue and renew licenses. The Department also establishes the administrative rules, conducts investigations, and engages in license enforcement as discussed in Chapter 5. The Department performs office services, and managerial, administrative, and budgetary functions for the Board. The Board and the Department work together in developing and approving examinations.

Real estate schools, courses, and continuing education programs require Department approval.

B.   LICENSING ISSUES

1.B.1   In Michigan, who is required to hold a real estate license?

Michigan real estate licenses are regulated under the Occupational Code (Public Act 299 of 1980). Under the Code, any individual or business, that engages in real estate for another for a fee as a principal vocation, or primary job, is required to hold a license. The state takes this authority under the concept of police power, which is the right of the governing body to enact laws to protect the public. A real estate agent is in a position to assist or harm the public; hence the need for licensing.

Anyone who, while acting for others for a fee, lists, buys, or sells real estate, or provides market analyses is required to be licensed, as is any person who is attempting these activities unsuccessfully. Working for others for a fee to rent real estate or to sell or exchange their business property, including the opportunity and the goodwill, also requires a license. Similarly, anyone who negotiates for the construction of a building on the real estate or negotiates real estate related mortgages is required to have a real estate license, unless that person is specifically licensed or registered under another law that would allow that person to perform those activities (see 1.B.3 below).

The state also stipulates that certain activities are by their very nature a principal vocation and so require a license. Acts constituting a principal vocation are

- engaging in more than five sales in any 12-month period;
- holding oneself out to the public as being principally engaged in the sale of real estate; or
- spending more than 15 hours per week, or more than 50% of one's working time, in any six-month period, in the sale of real estate.

1.B.2   What is the largest exception to the licensing requirements?

The most important exemption is for the person who acts on his or her own behalf. Any person can list, buy, rent, or sell, or name a person under a recorded power of attorney to do it on his or her behalf. The state does not regulate such a transaction: if the owner makes a mistake, the owner may only blame himself/herself, no one else. Also, by extension, **anyone who is employed by the owner of the property (on a regular full-time basis)** is exempt from having to be licensed to buy, sell, or manage property owned, rented, leased, or to be acquired by this owner.

1.B.3   Are there any other exemptions to the licensing requirements?

Yes, the law also exempts a court-appointed person, such as a receiver, trustee in bankruptcy, administrator, executor, or someone selling under a court order. A trustee, selling under a deed of trust, is exempt as long as the trustee does not engage in repeated sales. However, if any of these activities become a principal vocation, they will no longer remain exempt.

A person who performs real estate related activities but is separately licensed or registered for that particular activity does not need to be licensed as a broker or salesperson. Those persons who are exempt under this standard are

- a Michigan-licensed residential builder who is selling 1–4 housing that he or she has built, and that has never been occupied;
- an attorney at law while engaged in his or her professional capacity; and
- a Michigan-registered mortgage broker, lender, or servicer.

1.B.4   Does Michigan recognize licensure in other states?

Michigan does not recognize licensure of other states. Each licensee and educational program must conform to the Michigan requirements. A licensee from another state should contact the Michigan Department for specific guidance.

1.B.5   How does a corporation or partnership receive a real estate license?

A broker's license may be issued to a natural person, that is, an individual, or to an artificial person or business such as a sole proprietorship, partnership, association, corporation, or common law trust.

The broker's license is the only type of license that an artificial person (business entity) can hold. When the broker's license is granted to an artificial person, the state requires that at least one natural person act as a principal associate broker. The principal associate broker is responsible for ensuring the company's compliance with the licensing law and is entrusted with all of the obligations of an individual broker. The requirements for obtaining an associate broker's license are the same as for obtaining a broker's license, except that an associate broker must be a natural person.

Although there is only one type of associate broker's license, there are two categories of responsibility within the associate broker's license: the principal associate broker and the nonprincipal associate broker. A principal associate broker is an owner, partner, officer, or member of the real estate company and is responsible for the company's activities as noted above. A nonprincipal associate broker is a person who is not an owner, partner, officer, or member. A nonprincipal associate broker has the same duties as a salesperson, but has the additional ability of being a primary signatory on the broker's trust account and can also sign closing statements.

1.B.6   What is the difference between a salesperson and a broker? Can there be more than one broker in any given office?

The practices of the real estate industry are similar to the master craftsman/apprentice system of years ago. Real estate licensees usually start out with a salesperson's license working under the direct supervision of a broker. Michigan law requires that a person have the equivalent of three years of full-time experience in real estate or in a relevant, related field before being eligible to receive a broker's license.

There is only **one** broker's license in any company, although where the broker's license is granted to an artificial person, there may be more than one principal associate broker running the office. When the license law refers to a broker's obligations, it is referring to the individual broker or the principal associate broker. The other people in the office may hold salesperson's or associate broker's licenses.

The individual broker or principal associate broker may be the owner or a manager. The individual broker or principal associate broker is responsible for the trust account and for the real estate activities conducted by the associates in this office. A principal associate broker has all of the same responsibilities that an individual broker has under the law. An associate broker that is not a principal has the same responsibilities and privileges that a salesperson has, including the right to transfer his or her license. Nonprincipal associate brokers can also be the primary signatories on the trust accounts and can sign the closing statements, but salespeople cannot do either.

The public has the right to know that there is a person in charge locally. If a branch office is in another city that is more than 25 miles from the city limits in which the main office is located, the branch office is required to be under the direct supervision of an associate broker. The principal is still responsible for the trust money held by that office and the activities of each person licensed in that office. All service provision agreements are in the name of the broker, that is, the name of the company, not the individual.

1.B.7   What are the basic requirements to obtain real estate license?

An applicant must be at least 18 years of age and of good moral character. No formal education or experience is required to become a real estate licensee in Michigan. However, prelicensing education and testing are required to test for the applicant's competency (discussed below). In order to have good moral character, a licensee must have a propensity to serve the public in a fair, honest, and open manner. The applicant does not have to be a U.S. citizen or Michigan resident.

1.B.8   What are some reasons that the Department may deny a license?

A broker's license will not be issued to a new applicant who has been convicted of embezzlement or misappropriation of funds in the past. A person who has been denied a license may petition the Department for a review.

Additionally, applicants who have been convicted by a court of competent jurisdiction of any crime involving moral turpitude, such as forgery, embezzlement, obtaining money under false pretenses, theft, extortion, conspiracy to defraud, or similar offense, may have a difficult time proving that they have good moral character. An applicant who makes a false statement of any material fact on an application can be denied a license.

1.B.9   Will the Department make any exceptions to the educational and examination requirements?

No specific exceptions to the education requirements exist. However, broker's prelicensure credit equivalent to 60 clock hours of real estate education including six hours of instruction in civil rights and fair housing law is given for

- possession of a law degree obtained prior to the date of license application, and
- possession of a master's degree in business administration obtained from an accredited institution of higher learning.

A written examination is still required.

Exceptions to the written examination requirements are granted to an applicant for

- a salesperson's license who has held a salesperson's, associate broker's, or broker's license in the last three years; or
- an associate broker or broker's license who has held an associate broker or broker's license in the last three years; or

- an associate broker or broker license who surrendered his or her associate broker's or broker's license and has been continually licensed as a salesperson since that time.

An applicant who qualifies under the Americans with Disabilities Act is not exempt from the examination requirements but may request reasonable accommodations to the written exam.

1.B.10 Are there any special duties imposed on brokers and principal associate brokers?

A broker is employed by a member of the public, whereas a salesperson and associate brokers will always be licensed under a broker. The broker's duties to the public are direct, whereas a salesperson's or associate broker's duties are indirect.

A broker must maintain a physical place of business in Michigan where books and records are maintained. The broker or principal associate broker is responsible for ensuring that all the provided real estate related preprinted documents and forms are legal, correct, and current. The broker or principal associate broker is also responsible for the trust account.

1.B.11 Do the affiliated salespeople and associate brokers have any responsibilities?

Each actively licensed associate broker and salesperson must be licensed under a broker. In addition, a Department rule requires that each salesperson and associate broker keep his or her broker or principal associate broker fully informed. A licensee who fails to do this could be subject to disciplinary action.

1.B.12 Can a salesperson or associate broker be licensed under more than one broker?

No, a salesperson cannot be licensed under more than one broker during the same time period. A nonprincipal associate broker may only have one nonprincipal associate broker's license at the same time. However, he or she may concurrently be a nonprincipal associate broker for one broker and be a principal associate broker for another broker. Moreover, in the situation of a licensee who hires a licensed personal assistant, both must be licensed under the same broker. Only the broker under whom an assistant is licensed can pay the assistant for activity requiring a license.

A principal may hold multiple associate broker licenses. An individual may hold an individual broker's license and a principal associate broker's license at the same time. For example, John Smith may hold the following licenses at the same time:

- *Individual broker*—John's license will be issued to "John Smith, Individual Broker."
- *Nonprincipal associate broker*—John's license will be issued to "John Smith, Associate Broker." This license will also identify the employing broker, that is, the name of the company that John works for.
- *Principal associate broker*—John may concurrently be a principal in a variety of real estate ventures, such as Smith Realty Inc. and Smith Property Management LLC. John's licenses will be issued to "John Smith, Principal Associate Broker." The business entities, Smith Realty Inc. and Smith Property Management LLC, will each hold broker's licenses. John's principal associate broker licenses will each identify the employing broker.

1.B.13 What are specific requirements for an applicant to obtain a salesperson's license?

Qualified applicants for licensure as a **salesperson** must successfully complete a Department-approved course in real estate principles and practices of at least 40 clock hours of classroom time. At least four clock hours must cover civil law and equal opportunity.

After course completion, the candidate may take and pass the state-required real estate examination. The results of the examination are valid for 12 months (one year).

1.B.14 What are the additional requirements to become a broker?

A broker must have the equivalent of three years of full-time experience in real estate or in a relevant, related field before becoming eligible to receive a broker's license. A broker must have a physical Michigan location where he or she does business and the books and records are maintained.

The broker license applicant must complete, within the preceding 36 months, at least 90 clock hours of instruction, of which at least 9 clock hours is on civil rights and equal opportunity in housing. The 36-month period is extended if the applicant has held a salesperson license during the intervening period. The 90 hours are in addition to those hours required to obtain a salesperson's license. The 36-month period is waived for anyone who has received a master's degree in business administration or a law degree.

A broker applicant may be given credit for experience according to the following standards:

- *Salesperson or broker*—One year of credit for each 12-month period of licensure in which the applicant has engaged in six or more real estate transactions
- *Builder*—One year of credit for each 12-month period in which six residential, commercial, industrial, or combination units were built and personally sold
- *Investor*—Six months of credit for each five transactions personally negotiated for his or her account, with a maximum credit of one year (No credit is granted where there have been more than five sales in any 12-month period in violation of the principal vocation rule.)
- *Land or condominium developers*—One year of credit for each two developments of 10 units or more in which the applicant has bought, subdivided, and made improvements to the development
- *Attorney*—One year of credit for each year in which the applicant has conducted six real estate transactions
- *Related occupations*—One year of credit for each period in which the applicant has worked 40 hours per week, 48 weeks per year, in a decision-making capacity in a business directly related to the acquisition, finance, or conveyance of real estate. Related occupations include the positions of loan or trust officer in a federal or state regulated depository institution or mortgage company; real estate officer of a corporation that is not a real estate broker; officer at a title insurance company engaged in real estate closings; and staff or real property appraiser.

1.B.15 Who administers the real estate exam?

A Department-contracted provider, Applied Measurement Professionals (AMP), Lenexa, KS, conducts the real estate examination via computer by appointment. AMP offers computerized testing through a network of testing centers. The test is made up of 130 questions (salesperson) and 135 questions (broker) relating to Michigan licensing laws and general real estate principles and practices. The passing scaled score is 70 (not percent).

The *computerized* examination is designed to establish the competency of the applicant in order to protect the interests of the public. So long as the Department provides a uniform, standardized exam, the Department is only required to provide the examinees with a pass or fail notice. A breakdown of the raw data (number right) in each area is provided to those who fail the exam.

1.B.16 Who pays for the exam?

The candidate pays the examination fee ($46) directly to the testing service before being scheduled for an exam. If the applicant fails to appear, the examination fee is forfeited. If reexamination is required, another full examination fee is charged.

1.B.17 May a candidate who fails the exam retake it?

A person who fails to pass the real estate exam is allowed to immediately retake the exam by telephoning or filing a new registration form with AMP and paying the examination fee. There is no limit to the number of times that the applicant may take the exam.

1.B.18 What is the next step after one passes the exam?

Candidates are provided their pass/fail results on the day of the examination. If a candidate passes the examination, he or she will be provided with a Department-approved license application at the testing center on that same day. The Department will process the application to verify that all licensing requirements have been met and then issue the license.

If the Department determines that it is unable to issue the candidate's license within two weeks from when the Department determines that the candidate has met all requirements, then the Department must provide a temporary license to the candidate. Licensees cannot transfer on a temporary license. Candidates who pass the exam must file for a license within one year or the passing test results are nullified and the exam must be retaken.

A licensee's application must specify the time period that the licensee has been engaged in the business of real estate. Both the applicant and the employing broker or associate broker must sign the application for a salesperson's license. An application for a broker's license to be issued to a business entity must designate the individuals who will be acting as principals (associate brokers) and must be signed by an officer, owner, or member of the business.

1.B.19 How are license fees determined?

License fees are determined by the Michigan legislature and are paid annually. Expiration date of the license is determined by rule. Licenses currently expire on October 31 of each year.

Currently (2002), the fee for a new annual salesperson license is $23. The new annual broker or associate broker license costs $38. Legislation is pending that would increase the licensing fees and change the licensing term. For up-to-date requirements, please consult the Department's Web site.

1.B.20   Can the first time applicant ask for an inactive license?

No, Michigan law does not provide for an inactive license. An active license may be placed with a broker who will act as a private holding company. The licensee should have an agreement with the employing broker holding company that he or she will be inactive. However, as far as the Department is concerned, these licensees have active licenses.

1.B.21   Are there any residency or citizenship requirements?

In Michigan, there are no residency requirements or any United States citizenship requirement. Legal aliens can become licensed real estate agents in Michigan.

A nonresident of Michigan must file a Consent to Service of Process (BCS/LRE-900), an irrevocable consent to service of process allowing legal action to be brought against the nonresident in the state of Michigan. An applicant who has been licensed in another state must provide a current letter of good standing from that state's licensing division.

1.B.22   Does the Board do a credit check?

There are no credit check requirements for real estate licenses. However, the Board may request an independent source of information regarding previous occupation and criminal record.

1.B.23   What is the difference between a license and a pocket card?

The real estate license is a document issued by the Department that is approximately 5″ by 7″ in size. The license must be conspicuously displayed in the employing broker's office.

The pocket card is a wallet size replica of the license. The pocket card operates as the licensee's portable proof of licensing. The pocket card must be carried while transacting business.

1.B.24   How may a license be transferred from one office to another?

An individual broker's or principal associate broker's license cannot be transferred. This license must be surrendered to the Department, and a new license must be applied for. Similarly, a broker or associate broker cannot convert that license into a salesperson's license, or vice versa, but may surrender the one license and apply for the other. Brokers and principal associate brokers may have more than one license at the same time.

Salespersons and nonprincipal associate brokers may use a transfer process that allows them to continue to be licensed without interruption. To use the transfer procedure, a licensee must complete the transfer application and have the new broker endorse his or her license number on the back of the pocket card along with the date and the broker's signature. Upon the Department's receipt of the completed transfer application, the fees, and the old license, the endorsed pocket card will evidence licensure for 45 days from the latest date endorsed on the card.

If the application is incomplete, or if the broker to whom the licensee is transferring is not licensed, the pocket card becomes void and the transferee cannot operate until the new broker receives the new license. The ability to operate under the endorsed pocket card is subject to the Department's receipt of a transfer application within 45 days of the date endorsed on the card.

1.B.25 What are the procedures for transferring a license if the salesperson or associate broker quits or is fired?

If the salesperson or associate broker is fired, or quits by providing written notice, the broker has five days to deliver or mail (by certified mail) the license to the Department. If the salesperson or associate broker has not notified the broker he or she is leaving, the copy of the transfer form that the Department sends to the broker will operate as notification.

When a broker is returning a licensee's license to the Department, the broker must notify the licensee of the fact, in writing, to his last known address. The broker must send a copy of the notice to the Department with the license. The licensee must either return the pocket card to the Department, or mail a transfer form to the Department indicating that the licensee is keeping the pocket card under the terms of the transfer procedure. A licensee who has not transferred and whose license has been returned to the Department is unlicensed and cannot work as a salesperson or associate broker.

1.B.26 What happens if the license of the principal broker is suspended or revoked?

When a broker that is a business entity loses its only principal associate broker, the broker's license is suspended until a new principal is found. When a broker's license is suspended or revoked, all associate broker's and salesperson's licenses are suspended pending a change of broker and the issuing of a new license. The new licenses will be issued for the same term without an additional charge. The suspension or revocation of a broker's license will also terminate any branch office licenses held by the broker.

1.B.27 How is a license renewed?

Renewal applications are mailed to brokers and associate brokers in July and to salespersons in August. However, failure to receive the renewal notice does not relieve the licensee of this duty to renew. The licensee must submit the application form and pay the appropriate renewal fee.

Renewal applications must be returned to the Department with a check or money order by October 31. The Department has just begun a limited paper-less renewal option that allows individual licensees to renew online and pay the fee with a credit card. The current fee schedule is as follows: brokers and associate brokers, $18 and salespersons, $13.

1.B.28 How many continuing education (CE) hours are required for active status renewal?

The licensee must take six clock hours of CE within the 12 months previous to annual expiration. The licensee must take a course that is Department approved for the particular year that the licensee wishes to renew. Continuing education courses cannot be applied toward broker's license education requirements and vice versa.

1.B.29 Is there any alternative to attending continuing education classes for renewal purposes?

Yes, in the first year that a salesperson or broker receives an original license, he or she is exempt from continuing education requirements.

1.B.30 What are the consequences if the license is not timely renewed?

A licensee who has met all of the renewal requirements (that is, taken contin-uing education and mailed the renewal form and renewal fee) by October 31 may continue to operate under the expired license while waiting for the new license to arrive.

A licensee who misses the October 31 deadline may pay an additional $20 late fee and apply for late renewal within 60 days. An applicant for renewal who has missed the October 31 deadline cannot operate until the broker receives the new license and pocket card. In other words, the grace period is **to renew,** but **not to act.**

1.B.31 What if the applicant's check is returned for insufficient funds?

If a bad check is received for renewal of a license, a license will not be issued until the fee is paid.

1.B.32 How can a person whose license lapsed within the last three years reactivate the license?

A licensee whose license has lapsed may apply for a new license within three years of the last expiration date (relicensure) by meeting the current continuing education requirements. The applicant does not have to retake the exam or meet other additional educational requirements. Completion of continuing education for relicensure shall not qualify as completion of continuing education for the next license renewal.

1.B.33 How can a person whose license has lapsed more than three years ago reactivate the license?

The licensee may retake and pass the current exam in order to qualify for a new license. Alternatively, the applicant can avoid the exam if he or she took continuing education courses each year of inactive licensure or retakes an approved salesperson's 40-clock hour course.

1.B.34 Is there any way to reinstate a previously revoked license?

Yes, a previously revoked license may be reinstated, but no less than three years after the date of final revocation. In order to qualify for a new license after a revocation, the applicant must meet all education, examination, and experience requirements anew. No credit is given for education or experience acquired prior to the revocation.

C. LICENSEE DUTIES AND RESPONSIBILITIES

1.C.1 Who is responsible for each license?

A salesperson's or associate broker's license is mailed to the employing broker and must remain in the broker's custody and control. The broker is required to display all licenses in a conspicuous location in the broker's place of business. Each licensee is responsible for maintaining active licensure and for fulfilling renewal duties.

1.C.2 Is it legal for a licensee to buy and/or sell property for his or her own portfolio?

The licensee is not allowed to act in a dual capacity of both an agent and an **undisclosed** principal in any transaction. Without disclosure, there is a conflict of interest and an appearance of impropriety. Before buying real estate in

Michigan, licensees must give written disclosure to all parties of any ownership or interest that they have or will have in the transaction. The licensee cannot collect a commission unless the seller has agreed in writing.

A created *conflict of interest* should be discussed with both the seller-client and the buyer-client prior to an offer being made by the buyer or prior to an acceptance by the seller. Thus, licensees should purchase property from seller-clients or sell property owned by them to buyer-clients **only if** the licensee includes a clearly written disclosure describing the licensee's true position to the other party.

The administrative rules require a licensee to disclose his or her licensure when buying or acquiring, directly or indirectly. Therefore, by extension, a written disclosure is required when the licensee acts on behalf of the brokerage or any organization or business entity in which the licensee has an interest. The duty of disclosure may also extend when the licensee acts on behalf of a member of the licensee's immediate family.

1.C.3 May licensees sell or buy property for themselves without going through their brokers?

Affiliated licensees may buy for their own accounts. In Michigan, by administrative rule, licensed salespersons or associate brokers are allowed to sell only their own principal residence without the services of a broker. If no brokerage fees are to be paid and it is strictly a "by owner" transaction, where the licensee does not function as a licensee in any capacity throughout the transaction, then a licensee could advertise his or her own principal residence without including the name of the broker.

However, when selling all property other than their own principal residences, licensees must advertise in the name of the listing broker. Brokers or associate brokers may advertise their properties in their own names without listing them with the company, but must indicate that the seller is a licensed broker or associate broker in the ad.

1.C.4 Under what conditions may a real estate licensee hire a support person (personal assistant)?

Many licensees hire support persons to assist them. These assistants may be licensed or not licensed. Any brokerage that allows an affiliated licensee to employ support personnel (personal assistants) must implement a written company policy and procedures authorizing the practice. The written policy should include the prescribed duties that the support personnel may perform on behalf of the affiliated licensee.

1.C.5   Who is legally responsible for the activities performed by the personal assistant?

While not specifically addressed in Michigan law, affiliated licensees who engage personal assistants generally have the primary responsibility for their supervision. Obviously, the firm or sponsoring broker has supervisory responsibilities for the acts or activities of all licensees, including personal assistants.

1.C.6   What are some of the activities that an unlicensed person may perform?

While not directly addressed by Michigan law, it would appear that unlicensed assistants may perform general clerical and bookkeeping activities under the direct supervision of a licensee. Such permitted activities include answering the telephone and forwarding calls from the public to a licensee. An unlicensed assistant could schedule an open house, perform physical maintenance, and **accompany** a licensee to an open house or a showing and function as a host or hostess, so long as the assistant does not provide any real estate information. In addition, the unlicensed assistant is allowed to receive, record, and deposit security deposits and advance rents.

Unlicensed assistants generally may also perform the following duties:

- Submit listing data to the multiple-listing service
- Check on the status of closing files
- Assemble documents for closing
- Have keys made
- Write advertisements for approval by the licensee
- Place signs on property
- Act as a courier
- Schedule appointments with the seller or seller's agent in order to show the property
- Arrange dates and times for inspections, mortgage applications, walk-though inspections, and closings
- Hand to the public preprinted property information that has been prepared by a licensee

1.C.7   What activities are specifically prohibited for an unlicensed assistant?

Michigan laws prohibit any unlicensed person from prospecting by telephone or in person for listings, leases, buyers, 1031 exchange candidates, or property management contracts. In addition, unlicensed assistants are prohibited from hosting open houses, kiosks, home show booths, or fairs **independent** of their licensed employer.

Showing property without the licensed employer present is strictly prohibited. Other than the time and place of a closing, answering any real estate related question germane to the actual transaction is prohibited. Also prohibited are any negotiating or agreeing to commission structuring and the **collecting or holding** of deposit money or anything of value from either party.

One final note, just to clarify: unlicensed personal assistants are not allowed to hold themselves out in any manner as being licensed or affiliated as a licensee with a particular firm or real estate business. In other words, they are not allowed to print their names on real estate company business cards in an attempt to deceive the public.

2 Operating a Real Estate Business

The holder of a broker's license may open and operate a real estate business. The broker or principal associate broker may hire those holding either salesperson's or associate broker's licenses, although the broker or principal associate broker is ultimately responsible for the actions of affiliated licensees. This chapter covers the additional rules and regulations for brokers regarding advertising and trust accounts. Additionally, real estate licensees must comply with state variations from federal laws. These variations regarding federal Fair Housing and Megan's laws are noted.

A. OFFICE LICENSES

2.A.1 What licenses are required before a broker can open an office?

A person planning to open a real estate office must hold a broker's license. If a sole proprietor owns an office, the proprietor must be licensed as an individual broker.

If the office is to be owned by a legal entity, such as a partnership, limited liability partnership, corporation, or limited liability company, the entity must obtain the broker license and designate at least one partner, officer, member, or manager to act as its principal associate broker. The principal associate broker must be an individual who has met all of the criteria required to obtain a broker's license.

2.A.2   How does a corporation or partnership receive a real estate license?

When an individual broker, partnership, or other entity that chooses to operate under an assumed name owns the office, an assumed name certificate must first be obtained and submitted together with the broker's application.

When the office is owned by a legal entity, such as a corporation, limited liability company, or common law trust, an officer or member of the entity (i.e., an individual who has authority to act on behalf of the company) must execute the broker's license application. The entity must also designate at least one individual partner, officer, member, or manager to act as a principal associate broker. An application for a broker license to be issued to a legal entity must always be accompanied by an application for an associate broker license.

2.A.3   What is an assumed name certificate?

An individual or partnership operating under an assumed name obtains a certificate when it registers in the county in which it will be operating. Although a fairly rare occurrence, in Michigan a limited partnership, limited liability company, or corporation can also choose to operate under an assumed name. In this case, it receives a certificate of assumed name after registering with the State of Michigan, Department of Commerce, Consumer and Industry Services, Bureau of Commercial Services, Corporation and Securities Division.

Broker license applicants operating under an assumed name must submit a certificate of assumed name with the broker's application. The legal entity must submit a certificate of its enabling document, such as articles of incorporation or articles of organization.

2.A.4   How many licenses must a branch office have?

Where there is more than one office within Michigan, the additional offices must obtain a branch office license as the broker license. An associate broker must supervise a branch office that is located more than 25 miles from the city limits in which the main office is located. (Note that the requirement states 25 miles from the city limits, not from the main office location.)

An associate broker is not required for branch offices that are located within the same city, even if the branch is located more than 25 miles from the main office. This situation may occur in large urban cities, such as Detroit. The associate broker is not required to be a principal. There can be an unlimited number of licensees at each branch office, and there may be an unlimited number of branch offices.

B.   ADVERTISING RULES

2.B.1   What is a blind ad? Is it legal in Michigan?

In Michigan, a blind ad is one where a brokerage firm or listing agent includes just the broker's or agent's own name or a post office box number or a telephone number in order to bait readers into believing that the advertised property is offered by a private party. This unscrupulous practice is illegal in Michigan.

All brokers, when advertising real estate business, must use the broker's name as licensed and unmistakably indicate that the party is a real estate broker and not a private party. In addition to the broker's name as licensed, the ad must also include the broker's phone number or street address. Real estate advertising must be honest. It should never be misleading, deceptive, or intentionally misrepresent any property, terms, values, or policies and services of the brokerage.

Brokers can only advertise property under their own names if they are the owners, but even then they must indicate that they are brokers. Salespeople may sell their own principal residences themselves, but must list all other types of property with a broker. Therefore, salespeople can only advertise their own principal residences in their own names, but any advertisements involving the sale of a second residence or investment properties must supervised by, and advertised in, the name of the listing broker. A salesperson may advertise property for rent in his or her name only if the salesperson is the owner of the property.

2.B.2   Are there special requirements for a real estate office to advertise on the Internet?

There are no special rules for advertising on the Internet, except those previously mentioned. However, anyone other than the owner who offers to list, buy, rent, or sell real estate in Michigan is required to be licensed in Michigan. That is, an out-of-state broker who reaches a customer or client in Michigan cannot perform real estate activities within Michigan without a Michigan license.

2.B.3   Under what circumstances may a brokerage place a FOR SALE sign?

Neither the Michigan license law nor rules address the placement of For Sale signs on the property. This is a contractual issue that must be addressed between the seller and his or her agent.

Many municipalities, however, do have ordinances that deal with placement of signs. Some ordinances will limit the size of the signs, or limit the time span that a sign may be present, but the Michigan courts strike down flat-out prohibitions as restraints on alienation that are in violation of the Michigan constitution.

2.B.4   Are there any special rules about offering a property as a prize in a lottery or game?

Yes. A lottery, contest, game, prize, or drawing cannot be used for the sale or promotion of real estate, if it involves an element of chance and consideration was required. So sellers and their agents may not sell chances with a residence as the prize.

A game or contest that involves an element of chance but no consideration is permissible. Sales incentives, such as free gifts and promotions, are allowed as long as they are uniform and across the board.

C.   TRUST ACCOUNTS

2.C.1   What is trust money, and what can a broker do with it?

Trust money is money that belongs to someone else. Every Michigan-based real estate brokerage firm that expects to handle funds belonging to others must maintain a common trust account, identified by the words *trust, custodial,* or *escrow account,* in which to deposit its earnest money.

A brokerage that is involved in property management activities may also maintain a separate property management account, which is also a type of trust account. In this section, the term *trust account* is used in the same manner as in the Michigan Occupational Code and administrative rules, that is, to refer to an account that is used primarily for earnest money, as opposed to a property management account. Property management accounts are discussed more fully below and in Chapter 3, Section D.

The broker can never commingle these funds with his or her own funds that are held in a business or personal account. Brokers must keep accurate account records and balances, which they must make available to the Department upon request.

2.C.2   Where can trust funds be located?

Trust accounts must be held in non-interest-bearing demand accounts. A demand account is one in which the depository institution must allow the immediate withdrawal of the cleared funds. Checking accounts are typically demand accounts.

Savings accounts are usually nondemand, i.e., banking regulations allow them to place a hold on funds even though the funds have already cleared. Although the law allows the withholding of the funds, most depositories choose to allow their customers immediate access to their funds.

2.C.3   How soon must trust funds be deposited?

A salesperson who receives trust funds must, upon receipt, pay the funds to the broker. All funds belonging to others must be deposited into the broker's trust account no later than **two banking days after the broker has received notice of the acceptance by all parties.** This dated instrument could be an offer to purchase, a rental agreement, a lease, an exchange, or even an option. The rule is similar for earnest money that has been paid to a third party escrowee (see 2.C.16 below).

2.C.4   How does the listing office handle the earnest money when another office is working with the buyer?

In the case of a cooperative sale, it is usually customary in Michigan to have the broker who is working with the buyer hold the earnest money deposit. The broker is required to retain and to account for these funds until the transaction is consummated (closed) or terminated.

2.C.5   What are the rules if the buyer wants to use a postdated check or a diamond ring for earnest money?

Michigan does not have specific rules on this matter. However, the broker should not accept postdated checks or anything other than cash or an immediately cashable check as earnest money unless that fact is communicated to the seller prior to the acceptance of the offer and is stated in the offer to purchase.

2.C.6   What are the rules governing a trust account?

Unless there is a written agreement to the contrary between all parties, trust accounts in Michigan are required to be non-interest-bearing. By Department rule, in no event shall a Michigan broker be paid interest earned on money held in trust for others by the broker.

This means that if the parties desire to earn interest on the earnest money, they must deposit it directly with a third party that is not a real estate broker, such as a title insurance company, stock broker, or banker. In addition, Michigan brokers may not invest money belonging to others in any type of fixed maturity account, security, or certificate.

The broker or an associate broker must sign checks drawn on a trust account. An additional signature may be added according to the broker's company policy. However, the broker or principal associate broker is still held accountable for all trust monies.

2.C.7   What is commingling of funds and why is it illegal?

By definition, **commingling** is mixing personal funds with those belonging to other people. The broker's personal funds are to be used solely for paying expenses directly related to the maintenance of the trust account. Any amount in excess of $500 is considered **commingling.**

The problem with excess personal funds in the broker's trust account is simple. If the broker commingled personal funds into this account and the IRS froze the broker's accounts, then the trust account would be frozen too. The same thing could happen if a sole proprietor owned the brokerage and the sole proprietor suddenly died after commingling personal funds into the trust account. The commingled brokerage trust account could end up in probate. In either event, all closings would be tied up for a considerable length of time. To avoid these potential problems the rules specify that brokers may not keep more than $500 of their personal funds in the trust account.

2.C.8   What may not be paid directly out of the trust account?

It should be noted that the broker should never use the trust account as his or her business operating account or for personal uses. Monies that may not be disbursed directly from this account would include salaries and normal business or operational expenses. The broker can pay company commissions or commissions to other companies from the trust account only after fully accounting for the funds received and disbursed in his or her record books and showing a transfer of the sum on the closing statements.

2.C.9   What is the procedure for disbursing trust funds?

As a general rule, funds are disbursed from the trust account prior to the closing with the informed written consent of all the parties. In the event of a dispute over the return or forfeiture of any earnest money or escrow deposit held by the broker, the broker is required to hold the deposit in the trust account until he or she receives written consent from both parties.

Alternatively, the broker will disperse the disputed money when a civil action determines to whom the deposit must be paid. As a final alternative, the broker may interplead the deposit with the proper court.

2.C.10   What is an example of money in and out of a trust account?

It is possible for a broker to place an earnest money deposit into the trust account and, at closing, transfer a check in the amount of the earnest money to the brokerage account in lieu of commission earned. For example, a broker listed a lot for a $1,000 commission. It sold for full price and a $1,000 earnest money check was written and deposited into the broker's trust account.

At closing, the owner of the property gave the broker written permission, by means of the purchase agreement and closing statement, to keep the $1,000 earnest money (located in the trust account) in lieu of the commission owed. The $1,000 earnest money held in the trust account, due and payable now as commission earned, must be promptly withdrawn and transferred to the broker's business account or the broker could be found guilty of unlawful commingling.

2.C.11   What procedures must the broker follow when the buyer and seller disagree as to how the earnest money should be distributed?

Earnest money must be disbursed at the consummation or termination of the agreement in accordance with the agreement signed by both parties. From time to time, however, the parties may disagree as to disposition. In this case, where the buyer and seller have made a claim, the broker must keep the disputed money in the trust account until the buyer and seller have settled the dispute in writing.

However, under certain conditions, the Occupational Code and administrative rules authorize the broker to release disputed earnest money without written consent. One example is when the broker is in receipt of a final judgment of the court directing the disposition of the deposit. Another example is when a civil action is filed to determine the disposition of the earnest money. At that time the broker may seek court authorization to pay the deposit into the court in order to extract himself or herself from the dispute (an interpleader action).

2.C.12   How soon do buyers get their earnest money back when they withdraw their offer before it was accepted?

Obviously, a written release is not required when a seller rejects an offer, or the buyer withdraws his or her offer before notification of acceptance, since Michigan law does not require the broker to deposit earnest money until notified that the offer to purchase has been accepted by all parties. In both events, the earnest money is returned to the buyer without delay.

In Michigan, it is customary for licensees to keep earnest money checks inside their transaction files until offer acceptance. If the offer does not result in a contract, then the earnest money check is simply returned to the buyer or tenant.

2.C.13   Can the broker take his or her money from the earnest money directly out of the trust account if buyer and seller agree, just before closing, to rescind the contract?

No, the broker may not take his or her fees directly from the trust account. Should a transaction fail to consummate, the broker under no circumstances is entitled to withhold any portion of the earnest money even though a commission has been earned.

For example, the sellers accept an offer for the sale of their home accompanied by a $2,000 earnest money check. After acceptance, the buyers ask the sellers to let them out of the contract due to an unexpected job transfer. The owners agree and tell the buyers they can have their earnest money back too. In this case, when the sellers accepted the buyers' offer a commission was earned; however, the listing broker cannot hold the earnest money hostage. The broker must return the earnest money as directed and look to the sellers for compensation for services rendered.

2.C.14   Is there any other information about keeping proper records of the trust account?

A broker may have as many trust accounts as he requires, but cannot keep more than $500 of his or her own funds in each account. The broker is allowed to keep some personal money in the account for the purpose of meeting minimum balance requirements and for the payment of service charges (which are business expenses and cannot be paid from trust funds). As previously mentioned, maintaining more than $500 of the broker's own funds in the trust account constitutes commingling.

2.D.15   Does the Department require any special bookkeeping functions?

All trust account records must be retained for a minimum period of three years from the date of inception of the records. At minimum, the broker's bookkeeping system must consist of two record systems.

At the very minimum, the broker must show the **chronological sequence** in which funds are received and disbursed. For funds received, the broker must document the date of receipt, date of deposit, name of the party who provided the funds, name of the seller, and the amount received. For funds disbursed, the record must include the date of the disbursement, the payee, check number, and the amount and purpose of disbursement. The broker must maintain a current running balance of the account(s) and make that available to the Department upon request.

The Department also requires that the information be broken down into a **single record** that shows receipts and disbursements as they affect a single, particular transaction between a buyer and seller or landlord and tenant. In the records of a single transaction, for funds received, the broker must include the names of both parties to the transaction, the property address and/or a brief legal description, the date, and the amount received. In this same file, the broker must account for the funds disbursed by noting the date, payee, check number, and the amount of the disbursement.

2.C.16   What about trust funds that are payable to third parties?

A broker may accept trust funds that are made payable to a third party escrowee, such as a title insurance company. The broker must pay the funds over to the third party within two banking days after the broker has been notified that an offer to purchase has been accepted by all parties.

2.C.17   May property management funds, that is, security deposits, be handled differently?

Brokers may engage in property management, that is, collect a fee for offering to lease or rent property that belongs to others. A property manager must use a property management employment contract and must keep detailed property management accounts.

Property management accounts are treated more leniently than standard trust accounts. This is because management funds are actively used for rent collection and to pay real estate expenses. There are no time limits for depositing funds, although a prudent licensee will deposit the funds in a timely manner.

Property management accounts may be interest bearing. The interest is allocated between the broker and owner according to the terms of the property management employment contract. Additionally, a nonlicensee may sign checks drawn on property management accounts.

However, the broker must still keep the funds separate, maintain accurate records, account for all funds, and remit the funds according to the terms of the property management employment contract. The broker must maintain a bookkeeping system showing the date of a transaction, from whom the money was received or to whom it was paid, and other information as may be required by the property management agreement. All records maintained by the broker are subject to Department inspection. Earnest money funds cannot be kept in this account, but must be maintained in a separate trust account as specified in the above sections.

2.C.18   Any special rules regarding tenants' security deposits?

Michigan license law or rules do not specifically address tenant security deposits. The Landlord and Tenant Relationship Act states that the security deposit belongs to the tenant unless the tenant abandons claim to it, or until the landlord obtains a money judgment. The landlord must place the deposit in a regulated financial institution and cannot use the money unless he or she first secures a surety bond with the secretary of state.

D.   FAIR HOUSING IN MICHIGAN

2.D.1   Has Michigan enacted fair housing laws similar to the federal fair housing laws?

Yes. In 1963, Michigan was proud to be one of the first states to provide equal protection on the basis of religion, race, color, and national origin and to create a constitutionally empowered Civil Rights Commission in its State Constitution.

Michigan has enacted the Elliott-Larsen Civil Rights Act of 1976 (PA 220 of 1976) and Michigan Persons with Disabilities Act of 1998 (PA 331 of 1976). The initial laws prohibited discrimination based on race, color, religion, and national origin. Subsequent acts and amendments have added sex, age, familial status, marital status, height, weight, and physical and mental disabilities to the original four protected categories.

2.D.2   What state agency is responsible for enforcing Michigan's Fair Housing Laws?

The Michigan Civil Rights Commission was created in 1963 to carry out the guarantees against discrimination. According to its Web site http://www.michigan.gov/mdcr, the Department of Civil Rights "works to prevent discrimination through educational programs that promote voluntary compliance with civil rights laws and investigates and resolves discrimination complaints. It also provides information and services to businesses on diversity initiatives, equal employment law, procurement opportunities and feasibility studies, and joint venture/strategic alliance matchmaking."

Civil rights complaints can be lodged with the Michigan Civil Rights Department within 180 days. The Michigan Civil Rights Commission investigates and holds hearing on the complaints. Additionally, private agencies engage in tracking enforcement. Civil action may be commenced in a state circuit court.

An inquiry about a male's marital status is permissible if it is for the purpose of a real estate conveyance. Senior housing, for persons 50 years old or older, in compliance with a local, state, or federal program, may inquire as to familial status and age.

E.   MEGAN'S LAW IN MICHIGAN

2.E.1 Are real estate agents under any obligations re Megan's Law?

Briefly, Megan's law requires that certain sex offenders, when released from prison, must register where they live with the local police. Michigan's version does not require a real estate agent to discover or to disclose any information about the location of sex offenders.

Agency Overview

B rokerage involves bringing together two consumers, buyer and seller or landlord and tenant, to enter into a contract to sell, buy, rent, or manage real property in exchange for a fee. The state regulates the actions by the broker and his or her affiliated licensees who work with consumers. Depending on the circumstance, the brokerage may work for a consumer-client or work with a consumer/customer.

Since the consumer relies on the real estate licensee for information, it is imperative that the consumer understands the type, if any, of the representation the consumer has with the real estate licensee. This chapter discusses agency concepts, agency disclosures, brokerage agreements, and antitrust laws.

A. AGENCY ISSUES

3.A.1 How is agency defined in Michigan?

In real estate transactions, agency means a relationship in which a real estate broker acts for or represents another by the other person's **express** or **implied** authority in a transaction. The relationship is built on mutual respect, trust, honesty, and promise keeping. One party, called the *client,* **delegates authority** to his or her agent, who in return, **consents to act** for that client.

3.A.2 By what authority does the agent act?

In the case of a seller-client, the seller could elect to sell his or her home without the services of an agent but instead elects to **delegate** the task to an agent.

The agent receives (from the seller) express **authority** to procure a buyer, and by **written authority** receives permission to put up a sign, use a lock-box system (in the owner's absence) to gain entry into the home, and be present during offer negotiations. However, the agent does not have authority to bind the seller to an offer. In Michigan, the seller and broker must enter into a service provision agreement in order to address fees for the services provided. (See below for more details about the service provision agreement.)

3.A.3   What is a special agency?

When the agent is hired to perform a specific task or transaction, a **special** agency is created. In the preceding scenario, the listing agent's authority is very limited. The listing agent is a special agent, that is, one who is hired for a short term and receives limited authority. Agency agreements, referred to as *service provision agreements,* spell out the agency relationship.

Even if all of the terms of the listing agreement are met, the seller's agent does not have legal authority to bind the seller to an excellent offer. In this case, even though a commission may have been earned, the seller's agent has no authority to bind the seller to the offer.

3.A.4   What is a general agency?

A general agency is created when the agent is empowered to represent the principal in a broad range of matters related to a particular business or activity. The general agent may, for example, bind the principal to any contract within the scope of the agent's authority. This authority does not allow the agent to perform all acts for the principal, just those acts for which he or she is has been given authority.

A property manager is typically a general agent for the owner. Likewise, a salesperson or associate broker affiliated with the broker is a general agent. The key terms are *long-term and broad authority.*

The type of agency that is created will depend on the amount of authority that the principal empowers the agent with. The amount of authority that is transferred from the principal to the agent can be ranked. The agent receives the least amount of authority in a special agency, a greater amount in a general agency, and the greatest amount in a universal agency.

3.A.5   What is universal agency?

A universal agent is empowered to do anything and everything that a principal could do by himself. The term *universal* relates to the whole, without exception. A universal agency is usually created through the use of a power of attorney. The person that has been authorized under the power of attorney is referred to as an *attorney in fact*. Real estate licensees seldom act as universal agents.

If a buyer or seller cannot attend a real estate closing, they can use a power of attorney to designate an attorney in fact to attend the closing and act on their behalf. The power of attorney is often granted to a spouse or co-owner. A real estate licensee who is offered this type of authority should take the responsibility very seriously.

3.A.6   *What are the various agency options that Michigan permits?*

The Department requires that all brokers have written operating policies and procedures for their office. The type of agency practiced by the brokerage must be specified in these policies and procedures. A single-agency office policy can allow for the representation of buyers only, or for sellers only, or it may allow the representation of either buyers or sellers, but not both in the same transaction.

Subagency may also be practiced. This occurs when two agents (brokers) represent the same principal. The second agent derives his authority through the first agent, thus a subagency is established.

Michigan law authorizes the use of disclosed dual agency provided the brokerage has a company policy permitting its use. Michigan also provides for the use of designated agency. Designated agency is a variation of dual agency that attempts to alleviate some of the conflicts that are inherent in the dual agency. In offices that use designated agency, one licensee represents the seller; another licensee in the same office represents the buyer. The relationship between each of the licensees and the consumer is that of a single agency. However, the relationship between the brokerage and the consumers is one of consensual dual agency. (More details follow.)

It is also possible for a broker to be involved in a real estate transaction in a nonagency capacity. This could occur where the broker acts as a finder and so obtains a finder's fee, or where he or she acts as a transaction coordinator, as expressed in 3.A.10 below.

3.A.7   *What is single agency?*

In single agency, the agent represents only one party in any single transaction. The agent owes fiduciary duties exclusively to one principal, who may be either a seller/landlord or a buyer/tenant. Any third party is a customer. A customer is a consumer who is not being represented by a licensee but for whom the licensee may perform ministerial acts.

A seller's agent is an agent who singularly **represents** the seller in a real estate transaction, sometimes referred to as the *listing agent*. The buyer is then considered the customer. A buyer's agent is an agent who singularly **represents** the buyer in a real estate transaction, who is often referred to simply as the *buyer's agent*. In buyer agency, the seller is the customer.

Many real estate transactions in Michigan are single agency. The listing company represents the seller, and the cooperating broker represents the buyer. This can occur where a buyer refuses to commit to a service provision agreement, or where the broker's office policy permits single agency for the representation of sellers only.

3.A.8   What is dual agency, and is it legal in Michigan?

Michigan law authorizes the use of *disclosed dual agency*. A dual agency policy allows the brokerage to represent both the buyer and the seller in the same transaction, provided that full disclosure is made. Dual agency is created when both parties to a transaction give *authority* to **one** licensee to represent both parties in the transaction. The practice is illegal without **informed** consent. Michigan also requires that licensees use an agency disclosure form.

3.A.9   What is designated or appointed agency?

In Michigan, seller-clients and buyer-clients may **designate** a supervisory broker or associate broker and **appoint,** in writing, one or more different licensees affiliated with the brokerage to represent one of them. These appointed agents work as single agents for either the seller or buyer, *to the exclusion* of all the other licensees within the brokerage. Therefore, two licensees (from the same real estate brokerage) end up representing opposite sides in a single real estate transaction. The supervisory broker must be licensed at the broker level and cannot be a managing salesperson.

Under the Michigan Occupational Code, a licensee acting as an appointed agent will not be considered a dual agent, unless the licensee personally represents both the buyer and the seller, but the broker and all supervisory brokers are considered to be disclosed consensual dual agents. Using appointed or designated agents is an effort to avoid the potential conflict of interests inherent in dual agency.

3.A.10   Can Michigan licensees assist consumers in a real estate transaction without representing the consumer (nonagency)?

Yes, the Michigan licensee can participate in a real estate transaction as a *transaction coordinator*. A transaction coordinator is a licensee who works with customers but is not acting in an agency capacity. This situation may occur when a seller refuses to allow subagency and/or when the buyer does not want representation.

3.A.11   What are the pitfalls of being a transaction coordinator?

A transaction coordinator is allowed to provide information but cannot give advice. It is difficult to work with a customer and not give any advice. Once the licensee starts advising a customer, then the licensee is at risk of creating an implied agency. The customer may believe that the licensee is representing him in spite of what the agency disclosure specifies.

3.A.12   Who is the customer in a real estate transaction, and what duties does the agent owe the customer?

Full fiduciary duties are only owed to an agent's principal. However, a licensee must still be honest, use good faith, and he or she must disclose material facts to all parties in the transaction.

A customer is a consumer of real estate related services who is not being represented by the licensee. It is easy to recognize who the customer is when the agent represents the seller. The buyer is the customer. However, if the agent represents the buyer, the customer is the seller. Hence, it may be easier to use the term *third party.*

While providing brokerage services to customers, licensees must do so **honestly** and **in good faith.** They must diligently exercise reasonable skill and care, and licensees must disclose all known material adverse facts except those material facts that have already been discovered or discussed. In addition, there is a duty to account for any customer's property that comes into the licensee's possession.

3.A.13   Who is the agent's client and what does the agent owe this client?

A client is a party to a transaction who has an agency agreement with the licensee for brokerage services. Another name for a client is the principal. The principal is the individual who hires and delegates authority to a broker to represent his or her interests. The principal can be the seller, landlord, buyer, or tenant.

3.A.14   What are an agent's duties and obligations to a client?

Once an agency relationship is created, the licensee owes certain fiduciary duties to his or her client in addition to the duties to a customer. A fiduciary has the character of a trustee and has a duty to primarily act for another person's benefit. Duties owed include loyalty, fidelity, confidentiality, care, obedience, accounting, disclosure, notice of material facts, and no self-dealing.

In Michigan, the agent is obligated to place the client's interest ahead of the interest of any other party **(loyalty),** unless to do so violates the law. The Michigan agent must also **disclose** to the client all information known by the licensee that is material to the transaction and that is not known to the client or could not be discovered by the client through a reasonably diligent inspection. The agent must also disclose any financial interests the brokerage has in the transaction. The agent must fulfill the instructions **(obedience)** within the scope of the agency agreement (unless they are unlawful instructions). Finally, the Michigan broker may not accept any fees from anyone other than his or her client without the full knowledge and consent of the client.

When a seller's agent uses his or her superior skill to help the seller arrive at a realistic listing price, develop a marketing plan, and negotiate offers, **reasonable care** is demonstrated. A buyer's agent demonstrates **reasonable care** by helping the buyer evaluate property values, financial alternatives, offer, and counteroffer.

The duty of **accounting** requires the recording and reporting of all funds received from or on behalf of the principal. State law requires too that these funds be deposited into the broker's trust account within two banking days after the broker receives notice of the acceptance by all parties. Obviously, as mentioned earlier, unlawful *commingling* is illegal. (*Conversion* is the illegal practice of spending commingled funds for personal use.)

3.A.15   *What is subagency, and is it legal in Michigan?*

A subagency occurs when both brokers in a cooperative transaction represent the seller, and the buyer is merely a customer. Where the selling broker does not represent the buyer, he or she can choose to proceed as either a transaction coordinator or a subagent of the listing broker.

A subagent is one agent working for another agent who has a contract with a principal. At one time, only sellers had service provision agreements with brokers and all brokers working with buyers were subagents of the seller. Legal changes occur slowly; many Michigan brokers still prefer seller representation and offer subagency as their office policy.

B. AGENCY DISCLOSURES

3.B.1 What is agency disclosure?

When representing parties in a real estate transaction, Michigan law requires licensees to obtain written agency disclosures. The written disclosure form, signed by the client or customer, verifies that the licensee has, in fact, discussed agency options with the potential buyer, seller, landlord, or tenant. The written agency disclosure statement must be made prior to any communication of confidential information, specific to that potential buyer or seller. A written agency disclosure is required in all transactions involving the sale or lease of one-family to four-family houses, condominiums, or building sites (vacant lots).

It is important to note that just disclosing the broker's company policy does not create an agency relationship. The disclosure merely makes known the different possible agency relationships, and specifies which of these relationships the parties have chosen. To create an express agency, the disclosure form should always be coupled with a service provision agreement such as a listing agreement or buyer representation agreement. Although an agency relationship is not required to show real estate listings, the client must create an express agency relationship before the agent can provide specific assistance, a client-level activity that requires an agency agreement between the client and the agent.

3.B.2 What is specific assistance?

Although the Michigan law does not use the term *specific assistance,* it is a phrase often used to mean any communication beyond casual conversation that leads to the discovery of confidential information. It means eliciting or accepting confidential information about someone's needs, motivation, or financial qualifications. With this knowledge, an unscrupulous agent could disclose the confidential information of a client to the other party in a real estate transaction, thereby compromising the client's bargaining position.

Specific assistance may include a casual open house showing or preliminary conversations concerning price range, location, and property styles, or responding to general factual questions concerning properties that have been advertised for sale or lease.

3.B.3 How is agency disclosure made?

The agency disclosure must be made in writing on a form that substantially complies with the form provided in the Occupational Code. It must be presented prior to the buyer or seller's communication of confidential information to the licensee. The form contains an explanation of all of the various types of agency relationships, even if they are not being offered by a particular brokerage. It also contains spaces where the broker may check the type of agency relationship that has been agreed upon. Finally, the potential buyer or seller and the licensee must sign the form.

The agency disclosure form is not a contract and does not create the agency relationship. It can only be used alone when the buyer or seller has opted for a nonagency relationship and the licensee will operate as a transaction coordinator. Even then, it is wise to use a formal agreement.

In order to create an **express** agency relationship, a service provision agreement must be used together with the agency disclosure form. If the buyer or seller has chosen designated agency, then in addition to the service provision agreement, a designated agency agreement must be used.

The designated agency agreement names the brokers that are authorized to be supervisory brokers, names the client's designated agent, and specifies that two separate designated agents who work for the same broker, but represent different parties, are not dual agents. The service provision agreement could include the agency disclosure provisions, along with any designated agency provisions. These agreements between the agent and the client or customer do not need to be contained in separate documents.

3.B.4   Do agency disclosures include agreements for broker compensation?

No, the obligation of either the seller or the buyer to pay compensation to a licensee is not determinative of an agency relationship. The broker's compensation is determined by an agreement between the parties, which is often the service provision agreement, and not by an agency disclosure.

3.B.5   Does the agency disclosure create any obligations on the part of the buyer or seller?

The disclosure is simply an acknowledgement that agency has been discussed with the consumer. The consumer signs the document as proof that the licensee has discussed various agency options, the associated duties of each, as well as the intended agency relationship between the parties. Thus, the buyer or seller is free to work with other agents, unless the service provision agreement states otherwise.

What is critical is that the disclosure does set obligations on the part of the licensee/agent. Specific assistance can be entertained anytime after a meaningful discussion of agency has taken place.

3.B.6   What about dual agency disclosure?

Many offices have a policy permitting dual agency *with informed written consent*. In a dual agency, the licensee must endeavor to remain impartial and not aggressively represent the interest of either party to the exclusion or detriment of the other party. Licensees can only act as dual agents with written consent of all the parties.

The possibility of dual agency must be discussed and agreed upon prior to the seller signing a listing agreement or before providing specific assistance to the buyer. If the consumer creates an agency agreement with the agent and agrees to the possibility of dual agency, then a second disclosure, together with client consent, may be required at the time that the agent actually becomes a dual agent.

3.B.7   What happens if no agency disclosure is made?

Failure to provide an agency disclosure is in violation of the license law and the licensee is subject to its penalties. An agency disclosure is separate from the creation of the agency relationship. The primary reason to provide an agency disclosure is to prevent the buyer or seller's mistaken belief that the licensee represents him when in fact he does not.

In spite of the licensee failing to provide an agency disclosure, an agency relationship may have been created. The creation of an agency relationship, whether expressly or by implication, also creates fiduciary obligations. The breach of a fiduciary duty to the principal, in addition to creating liability on the part of the licensee, will also cause the commission to be forfeited.

3.B.8   Are any other disclosures required?

Unless a written notice to the contrary exists, licensees are prohibited from accepting undisclosed compensation (related to the transaction) from any person other than the agreed parties. Also, licensees must disclose in writing when acquiring real estate on their own behalf, or indirectly such as on behalf of an immediate family member or brokerage, or on behalf of a business entity in which the licensee has an interest.

C.   BROKERAGE AGREEMENTS

3.C.1   What is brokerage?

A real estate broker is defined as a person licensed to buy, sell, exchange, or lease real property for others and to charge a fee for those services. As discussed in the previous chapter, Michigan requires a license to act as an agent, advertise one's services as an agent, negotiate, collect rents, or find prospects for real estate related activities.

3.C.2   What are brokerage or service provision agreements?

Brokerage agreements, also referred to as *service provision agreements,* are essentially employment contracts requesting the professional services of the licensee, not the transfer of real estate. Brokers enter into employment agreements with their affiliated licensees, with sellers, with buyers, with landlords, and with tenants. Brokerage agreements confirm compensation issues. It is not required that service provision agreements create an agency relationship in Michigan.

Depending on the agreement, the broker will be an agent or a principal. In the employment contract with affiliate licensees, the broker is the principal and the affiliate licensees are the broker's agents. Although not required by Michigan law to be in writing, the broker gives authority to the affiliated licensee to act on behalf of the broker in certain situations. Brokers are encouraged to detail the duties in a written agreement (see 3.C.3).

In a listing agreement, the seller is the principal (client) and the broker is the agent who "subs" the work to his agents (affiliate licensees) or other brokers (subagents). In a buyer brokerage agreement, the buyer is the principal (client) and the broker is the agent, again "subbing" the work to his or her affiliates.

3.C.3   What kind of agreement exists between a broker and the people who work for the broker?

Brokers enter into employment agreements with the licensees who work for the broker, thereby permitting the licensees to act as agents for the broker. Thus, even though a salesperson or associate broker may negotiate the service provision agreement, the agreement is in the name of the broker.

A broker is responsible for supervising the real estate activities performed by a salesperson or associate broker employed by or otherwise associated with the broker as a representative of the broker, even if the affiliate licensee is classified as an independent contractor. The salesperson or associate broker is responsible for keeping the employing broker fully informed of all activities being conducted on behalf of the broker and any other activities that might impact on the broker's responsibilities.

The Occupational Code specifies that a broker can only treat affiliated licensees as independent contractors if two conditions are met: (1) there is a written agreement in which the broker indicates that the associate broker or salesperson is not considered as an employee for federal and state income tax purposes, and (2) not less than 75% of the annual compensation from the real estate broker to the affiliated licensee is based on commissions earned, not hours worked.

3.C.4 What duties does the broker have to his or her affiliated licensees?

A broker or associate broker is required to supervise his or her licensees. The broker is expected to provide the affiliated licensees with written operating policies and procedures. Supervision also includes direct communication in person, by telephone or electronically, on a regular basis. It also means reviewing the licensee's practice and reports and guiding the performance of regulated activities.

3.C.5 Are referral fees legal in Michigan?

Every year real estate agents help thousands of families by referring them to other licensees across the United States. In return for the referral, a percentage or other agreed upon fee is paid back to the referring broker. These fees are legal if paid between licensed brokers.

3.C.6 What are the service provision agreements between the brokerage and consumers?

A service provision agreement sets forth the rights and obligations of both parties, and generally includes an agreement for broker compensation. These agreements are entered into by the brokerage with sellers, buyers, tenants, and landlords. The rules are the same whether the real estate is residential, commercial, industrial, or special purpose.

3.C.7 What are the various service provision agreements with consumers?

A seller hires a broker under a **listing** agreement. An agreement between a broker and a buyer is a **buyer brokerage** agreement. A **management** agreement is a contract between a property owner and the broker who is hired to manage the rental property.

Even if an affiliate salesperson or associate broker negotiates the agreement, the contract must be written on behalf of the employing broker and is still between the consumer and the broker. It is important to remember that the agency disclosure merely acknowledges disclosure; the aforementioned agreements address exclusivity and compensation issues.

3.C.8   What is a net listing and why is it illegal in Michigan?

A net listing, referred to as a *net service provision agreement,* is an agreement that specifies a net sale price to be received by the owner with the excess over that price to be received by the broker as commission. This situation presents a potential conflict of interest for the broker.

Often, the seller only realizes the true selling price of the property when an offer to purchase is obtained. Because of the appearance of impropriety between the fiduciary broker-client relationship and the broker's profit motive, the taking of a net service provision agreement is considered unprofessional conduct and constitutes a violation of the Michigan Occupational Code.

3.C.9   What are exclusive listings?

Exclusive right-to-sell listing agreements give brokerage firms the *exclusive right* to market the seller's property and receive a commission if the property is sold during the term of the listing, regardless of which person finds the buyer, including the owner. A variation is the exclusive agency listing in which the owner of the property promises to compensate a broker for locating a buyer, but the owner reserves the right to find his or her own buyer without paying the broker a commission. The listing agreement should clearly state if the agreement is an exclusive agency or exclusive right to sell.

Nonexclusive listings are referred to as open listings. Multiple brokers may be involved in the marketing of an open listing. The first broker to find a buyer would be the broker that is entitled to the commission.

3.C.10   What specifically must a listing agreement include?

To have legal recognition, all listing contracts in Michigan must be written. The listing agreement or service provision agreement with the seller must properly identify the property and the terms and conditions under which the property is to be sold. Specifically, the service provision agreement must include the listing price, the commission to be paid, the signatures of all concerned parties, and a definite expiration date. The service provision agreement must be fully completed before it is signed.

Michigan law specifically prohibits automatic renewal clauses in service provision agreements, and all service provision agreements must contain a definite expiration date. Agents are required to give a legible and fully completed copy of the agreement to the owner parties at the time of signing.

3.C.11   At what time may a listing broker place a FOR SALE sign on the property?

The seller and the broker determine the placement of signs. Many brokerages include specific authorization for a For Sale sign as part of the service provision agreement.

3.C.12   Who or what determines the brokerage fee?

A commission or fee in any service provision agreement is fully negotiable among the parties to that agreement. The service provision agreement must spell out the broker's commission amount. It can either be a percentage of the sale, an hourly fee, a flat fee, or a combination of these.

The seller, in the service provision agreement, may authorize the listing company to share compensation with other licensees, including a buyer's agent solely representing the buyer. Once the parties to an exclusive service provision agreement agree on the structure of the commission, no one is allowed to alter or attempt to alter the commission arrangement without obtaining the parties' prior written consent.

Although the Michigan Occupational Code and administrative rules are silent on the matter, licensees who **induce buyers** to write contracts that seek to alter commission arrangements, without the listing agent's prior written consent, may be accused of tortuous interference with a contract.

3.C.13   What is procuring cause?

Procuring cause in a real estate transaction means that a licensee started or caused a chain of events that resulted in the sale of a listed property. Procuring cause disputes happen between cooperative brokers and are normally settled by arbitration through local boards or associations of REALTORS®. The Department does not have jurisdiction over disputes between brokers as to fees and commissions.

3.C.14   Are there any other considerations that may be included in a listing agreement?

A listing agreement must contain language stating that discrimination based on religion, race, color, national origin, age, sex, disability, familial status, or martial status on the part of the real estate broker, salesperson, seller, or lessor (landlord) is prohibited.

3.C.15   Who must sign a service agreement?

In order to prevail in a court of law, a contract must be signed by the party to be charged with the contract. Therefore, the persons that have obligations under a service provision agreement are required to sign it.

3.C.16   What is a protection clause, and whom does it protect?

A protection clause, also known as an *extender,* or *carryover, provision* protects the broker from unscrupulous sellers or buyers who take the broker-generated leads and then buy or sell the property *after the service provision agreement expires* to avoid paying a commission to the broker. A protection clause can be included in either the buyer's or seller's service provision agreement, or both, and extends beyond the expiration of the agreement. The agreement must include the protection clause as part of the original agreement and must set a definite protection period.

At the present time, the use of protection clauses in a buyer service provision agreement is not specifically addressed in Michigan law. However, if used, the clause should include a definite protection time frame and state that at the expiration of the service agreement, if the buyer purchases, leases, or acquires any interest in any previously shown property by the licensee, then the buyer agrees to pay the agreed upon fee. It would be wise for the licensee to provide the buyer with a list of the names and property addresses for which protection is sought.

3.C.17   Can a broker solicit another broker's listing?

Legally binding, **exclusive** service provision agreements must be respected by outside parties. Alienating those involved in contractual relationships is the tortuous interference with a contract.

3.C.18   Can a salesperson who decides to work for a different broker take several listings to the new brokerage?

Upon the termination of employment, licensees are not allowed to take or use any service provision agreements secured during their employment with the first broker. Brokerage agreements are the property of the broker and can be canceled only by the broker and the seller, unless the terms of the contract state otherwise.

3.C.19   Can a licensee receive compensation from a former broker for listings left behind?

The Occupational Code allows a broker to pay earned compensation to a former licensee, even if the licensee is currently licensed to another broker, or if he is no longer licensed. Notice that the law states that this is allowed, not that it is required. Whether a broker is required to compensate a former licensee is an employment contract (independent contractor agreement) issue.

3.C.20   What does the brokerage agreement with a buyer have to include?

Listing agreements and buyer brokerage agreements are treated the same way under the department's administrative rules. Both types of agreements are referred to as *service provision agreements*. The buyer service agreement must have a specific termination date.

3.C.21   Does the agent owe the buyer-client anything after the termination of the relationship?

Legal and ethical implications of agency and certain duties of loyalty (confidentiality) may survive even after the termination of a buyer's agreement. Examples include accounting for moneys and property received during the contractual period as well as keeping confidentially requested information confidential.

3.C.22   Under what circumstances may a broker (or his or her agents) meet another broker's client?

As a matter of general agency law, listing agents should allow buyer's agents to accompany prospects at any step in a real estate transaction. However, a listing agent is not required to permit a buyer's agent to be present when presenting an offer to a seller-client or discussing confidential matters with the seller-client.

With the listing agent present, buyer's agents are sometimes afforded the courtesy to personally present their client's or customer's purchase agreement directly to the seller. If this courtesy is not extended, the buyer's agent must present the buyer's purchase agreement to the listing agent, and then the listing agent (singularly) presents the offer to the seller.

The Michigan Occupational Code and administrative rules do not specifically address this issue. Each brokerage firm or local REALTOR® board or association may create its own policies and procedures to handle this situation.

3.C.23   Do brokers have to cooperate and compensate each other?

Brokers recognize that while one brokerage has the listing, another broker may already be working with a buyer. The buyer wants to continue to work with the licensee he has chosen, not the listing agent. In this situation, the seller benefits from the listing broker agreeing to share the compensation with the other broker who actually procures the buyer.

This cooperation benefits the seller by opening the property to more potential buyers. Michigan does not require that the broker must cooperate with or compensate another broker. However, the listing agreement should specify the types of cooperation and compensation being offered. This disclosure is intended to inform the client of any policy that would limit the participation of any other brokerage. Additionally, if a broker has implied or indicated that he or she will cooperate, then he or she must cooperate.

D.   PROPERTY MANAGEMENT AGREEMENTS

3.D.1   What is a management contract?

A management contract, known as a *property management employment contract*, is between the brokerage and the property owner who wishes to lease real property but does not want to deal directly with tenants and the property. In Michigan, if a broker wants to become a property owner's authorized leasing agent, a current written property management employment contract is required.

The owner hires a real estate licensee to manage the property, that is, locate tenants, handle repairs, collect rents, and so forth. Michigan law requires that this contract for a broker's services be in writing.

3.D.2   What must be included in the management agreement?

The manager and owner spell out the structure of their relationship—their specific responsibilities and liabilities. A property management employment contract must specify the broker's duties, responsibilities, and activities as a property manager. It must include provisions for use of funds and their management, safekeeping, investment, and disbursement. Often, the broker is a general agent (see 3.A.4).

3.D.3   How are the owner's funds treated?

The rules are different for property management accounts than they are for earnest money trust accounts, discussed in Chapter 2, Section C. A broker must maintain management accounts separate from all other accounts, but the account does not need to be a demand account. This account may earn and distribute interest as specified in the property management employment contract. A designated employee of the broker may sign the checks without the broker's cosignature.

The broker must still maintain careful records of all funds deposited and withdrawn from the property management accounts. The records must indicate the date, from whom the money was received or to whom the money was given, and other pertinent information. These records must be maintained for a minimum of three years and are subject to inspection by the Department.

E.   ANTITRUST LAWS

3.E.1   Does Michigan have an antitrust law?

Yes, the Michigan Antitrust Reform Act (PA 274 of 1984) prohibits contracts and conspiracies to establish a monopoly of trade or commerce, for the purpose of limiting competition or controlling, fixing, or maintaining prices.

3.E.2   What activities are regulated by this law?

The law regulates several practices:

- *Price fixing*—an agreement made by competitors to set prices
- *Group boycotts*—a refusal to deal with competitors with the intent to force them out of the market
- *Customer allocation*—dividing a territory among competitors
- *Tying arrangements*—conditioning the purchase of one product or service upon the purchase of another, less desirable, service.

3.E.3   What type of activities are permitted?

Noncompetition agreements are permissible where they are reasonable in duration, geographical area, and the type of business.

3.E.4 What are the civil and criminal penalties under the act?

The attorney general or a prosecuting attorney may bring an action for injunctive or other equitable relief. The court may assess a civil penalty up to $50,000 for each violation.

In the event of immediate irreparable harm, a person may bring an action for injunctive or other equitable relief. A person may recover actual damages, interest on the damages from the date of the complaint, costs, and reasonable attorney fees. If the violation is flagrant, recovery may increase to three times the actual damages. The action may be brought in circuit court without regard to the amount in controversy.

Violation of the act is a misdemeanor. An individual can be imprisoned up to two years and/or fined up to $10,000. A business entity can be fined up to $1,000,000. A criminal prosecution cannot be brought if a prior criminal prosecution has been initiated under the Sherman Act (federal law) arising out of the same transactions.

3.E.5 What is the statute of limitations under this Act?

Civil action by the attorney general or a criminal prosecution must be initiated within four years. An action for damages must be brought within four years. If the action is based on the same issues as a civil or criminal action brought by the state, the time period may be extended to one year after the conclusion of the state action.

4 Contracts and Closings Overview

When preparing to make and accept offers for the sale or rental of real property, buyers and sellers want to make decisions based on full knowledge of the property and title. Additionally, in today's marketplace, the real estate industry has seen a movement from *caveat emptor (buyer beware)* to seller disclosure. Today, sellers are asked to disclose information material to a buyer making an informed decision.

The Michigan legislature has addressed these concerns. This chapter discusses disclosures covered by the Seller Property Disclosure, stigmatized properties, and certain environmental topics. It also considers contract issues including offers and acceptances and fraud. Closing concerns, including abstracting, and conveyance taxes are also discussed.

A. CONTRACT ISSUES

4.A.1 What is a contract?

A contract is a set of legally binding promises between two informed parties that must be performed and for which the law provides a remedy for any breach. For legal recognition, all agreements related to the transfer of Michigan real estate involving the sale of an interest in land, or where obligations will continue for longer than one year, must be in writing and signed by the party to be charged with the agreement.

In Michigan, upon execution of any instrument in connection with a real estate transaction, licensees are required as soon as practicable to deliver legible copies of the original document to each party. It is the responsibility of the licensee to prepare sufficient copies of such instruments to satisfy this requirement.

4.A.2   What is the age of legal competence in Michigan, with no exceptions, to enter a contract?

In Michigan a person is legally competent at age 18.

4.A.3   What does informed parties mean?

Before entering into a legally binding contract to buy or sell real estate, what the parties offer and accept must be the same. Hence, it is important that sellers disclose every important issue (material fact) about the property. Otherwise, the buyer is buying less than agreed upon. It is an act of fraud to withhold disclosure of material adverse facts. Sometimes, a seller or agent does not know and negligently withholds information. In these situations, the buyer may be able to void the contract.

4.A.4   What is a material adverse fact?

In Michigan, **material adverse facts** are those conditions or occurrences that are generally recognized as being of such significance that they would affect either party's decision to enter into a contract. Generally included in this definition are those situations that significantly and adversely affect the value of a property and those situations that significantly reduce the structural integrity of a property. Also, any situation that presents a significant health risk to the occupants of the property would be considered a material adverse fact.

This issue is so important that the Michigan rules specify that a licensee who discloses material facts to a customer will not be disciplined by the Department for disloyalty if his principal claims that he was in violation of the agency relationship.

4.A.5   What is fraud?

Fraudulent acts require intentional deception in such a way as to intend to harm another person. Several examples are fraudulent advertising, making false statements about a property's condition, and intentionally concealing known facts. Such fraudulent acts are subject to license suspension or revocation.

Silent fraud is a false impression that is created by silence, or failure to properly disclosure. There are too many Michigan cases in which a seller fails to advise a buyer of a material adverse fact and is later found liable for silent fraud.

4.A.6   What is negligence?

Misrepresentation or omission of pertinent facts does not have to be intentional to bring liability exposure. **Negligent misrepresentation** occurs when a licensee *knew* or *should have known* that incorrect statements were being relied upon as material fact.

Innocent misrepresentation occurs when a licensee makes incorrect statements but has reason to believe that the statements are true, as when a licensee answers a question about the property based on information contained in the Seller's Disclosure Statement. There are no cases in Michigan, to date, where an agent has been found liable for innocent misrepresentation.

4.A.7   Who is permitted to draw up real estate contracts?

Brokers and salespersons may complete standard forms printed by stationers when it is incidental to the brokering of the transaction, there is no additional charge, and no advice is given as to the legal effect or validity of the form.

Brokers may also prepare statutory deeds and closing statements in order to complete a transaction that they have brokered.

4.A.8   What specifically may a broker NOT prepare?

In Michigan, real estate brokers should be cautious to avoid the charge of practicing law without a license. They can only complete forms and transcribe language dictated by the principal.

Brokers are not allowed to prepare affidavits of child support or spousal support, or documents necessary to correct title defects. Licensed attorneys must be used for these documents.

4.A.9   How is property described in Michigan legal documents?

Most property in urban Michigan is described by lot and block referenced to a recorded plat at the register of deeds office in the county where the property is located. The measurements are surveyed using compass directions and linear feet. Once subdivisions are submitted for approval and recorded, plats are adopted for future legal descriptions.

In more rural areas, metes and bounds descriptions are common. For larger rural parcels, the government survey system is used.

4.A.10   Is a legal description required in a listing agreement?

There must be a *meeting of the minds* to make a contract, and the address must be definitive enough to have clarity on what is being sold. Michigan courts require that contracts, such as listing and purchase agreements, contain a legally sufficient description. An actual legal description, although preferred in a listing agreement, is not required as long as the property boundaries can be identified and it creates a meeting of the minds between the parties.

Street addresses are not considered legal descriptions because of their temporary nature. A street address can locate a property but not designate its boundaries.

4.A.11   What forms must be completed during a real estate transaction?

In addition to the purchase agreement, Michigan also requires the use of the agency disclosure. For the sale of residential properties, another form or two are required: the Seller's Property Disclosure and, if the residence was built prior to 1978, a lead-based paint disclosure form.

Michigan Department rules require every broker to deliver to the seller a complete detailed closing statement and, at the same time, a detailed closing statement to the buyer.

B.   SELLER'S DISCLOSURE STATEMENT

4.B.1   What is the purpose of the Seller Disclosure Act (PA 92 of 1993)?

The purpose of the act is to provide for a property disclosure statement that will forewarn prospective buyers of the condition of the property before writing an offer. If the procedures are not followed, then the buyer can revoke the offer.

The disclosure statement includes information about the property's plumbing, electrical, and heating systems, any significant structural defects, presence of pests, zoning violations, environmental issues, repairs made, common use areas, and farming operations. Section 7 of the Act provides a form that must be used for making discosures.

4.B.2   When must the property disclosure be made?

The written disclosure statement must be delivered before the transferor, usually the seller, executes a binding purchase agreement, or where there is no purchase agreement, before the transferor executes the installment sale contract. If it is delivered after the purchase agreement is signed, the buyer may rescind the purchase agreement as stated in 4.B.6.

4.B.3   To what properties does the Seller Disclosure apply?

A seller must provide the prospective buyer with a Seller's Disclosure Statement prior to the transfer of certain types of residential property. The law applies to one-family to four-family residential properties, including condominiums and cooperatives if they are being offered for sale or exchange. The act also applies where the sale is being made through an installment land contract, or where the transfer occurs through a lease with an option to purchase, any other type of option to purchase, or a ground lease coupled with proposed improvements.

4.B.4   What transactions are exemptions to the Disclosure Statement requirement?

Some property owners and/or transactions are exempt by law. Exempt transactions include those

- by court orders, including writ of execution, bankruptcy, eminent domain, and specific performance;
- to a lender by a borrower who is in default;
- occurring as a result of a foreclosure sale;
- by a nonoccupant fiduciary in the course of the administration of a decedent's estate, guardianship, conservatorship, or trust;
- from one co-owner to another co-owner;
- to a spouse, parent, grandparent, child, or grandchild;
- between spouses resulting from a judgment of divorce or a judgment of separation;
- to or from any governmental entity, and
- involving new construction that has not been inhabited and was built by a licensed residential builder.

4.B.5   Who must make the property disclosure?

The disclosure statement applies to any owner interested in transferring residential real property. The transferor is required to deliver a written disclosure statement to any person interested in being transferred the real property. Compliance with this law must be noted on the purchase agreement, installment sales contract, lease, or an addendum, or by a separate document.

The transferor's agent must make copies of the disclosure statement available to the potential transferee or his agent. Private sellers may obtain blank copies of the form from any real estate licensee.

4.B.6   What are the consequences if the disclosure is not made or is made after the offer has been accepted?

If the disclosure statement, or any amendment, is delivered after the transferor executes a binding agreement, then the transferee has 72 hours after the delivery to terminate the agreement. If the disclosure statement was delivered by registered mail, the time period increases to 120 hours after delivery.

4.B.7   After the seller filled out the property disclosure form, some items changed. How should these changes be handled?

If information disclosed becomes inaccurate after the delivery of the required disclosures, the resulting inaccuracy does not constitute a violation of this act. However, *in order to avoid allegations of misrepresentation,* the best practice is for the transferor to amend the disclosure statement in writing. Once an amended statement is delivered to the transferee, the transferee will again receive an opportunity to terminate the agreement as stated in 4.B.6.

4.B.8   What are the licensee's responsibilities to ensure that the seller makes the disclosure and that the buyer receives it in a timely fashion?

In Michigan, the **listing agent** is required to obtain a completed disclosure, signed and dated by each seller represented by the brokerage. Then, the licensee makes sure that the executed statement is delivered to either the potential buyer or buyer's agent before any offer is written. The listing agent then requests a signed and dated copy of the form before any offer is presented to the seller.

The **buyer's agent is responsible** for informing the buyer of the seller's obligation to deliver the property disclosure statement, and that without the buyer's signature and date, the sale could be negated based on the "without liability" rule. If the disclosure statement is delivered after a binding agreement has been executed, the buyer may withdraw the offer or revoke an already accepted offer "without liability" (see 4.B.6).

Delivery to the transferee's agent is deemed to be delivery to the transferee. Delivery or execution of a facsimile is considered to be delivery or execution of the original.

4.B.9   What if the property transfers without a seller disclosure statement?

A transfer is not invalidated solely because of a failure of a person to comply with the written disclosure requirement. A transferee who "closes" without having received a Seller's Disclosure Statement can no longer terminate the transaction.

4.B.10   What liability does the licensee bear regarding the Seller Property Disclosure form?

The transferor or agent is required to use ordinary care when filling out the form. Neither is liable for errors not within the personal knowledge of the transferor, or those based on information provided by other persons. An agent does not have liability for the transferor's violation of this law, unless the agent knowingly acts in concert with the transferor.

The transferor is not required to disclose information that could be obtained only through inspection of inaccessible portions of real estate or could be discovered only by an expert. A report delivered by a public agency or expert, such as a licensed professional engineer, professional surveyor, geologist, structural pest control operator, or contractor, relieves the transferor of any further disclosure with respect to that item of information. Of course, if the transferor has knowledge of a defect that contradicts the information provided, he or she must provide the information.

C.   OFFERS AND ACCEPTANCES

4.C.1   Does the listing agent have to let the buyer's agent present the offer to the seller client?

Although not specifically addressed by license law, a seller's agent is not required to permit a buyer's agent to be present when presenting offers or discussing confidential matters with the seller-clients. However, in some Michigan brokerage communities, it is customary to allow the buyer's agents to be present during the presentation, or to give buyer's agents the privilege of presenting their buyer's offer.

4.C.2   In what order are multiple offers presented to the seller for consideration?

Michigan Department rules state that any and all offers must be promptly delivered to the seller for consideration or the broker can face disciplinary action. The seller must be permitted to view all offers to determine which offer is best for the seller. Upon obtaining a proper acceptance, the licensee must then promptly deliver true executed copies to the buyer and seller.

Licensees need to help the buyer understand that another offer may be presented while the seller is considering the first offer. No particular courtesies are extended to the person writing the first offer. There is no particular advantage to writing the first offer.

4.C.3   Should subsequent offers be presented to the seller if other offers arrive after the seller accepts an offer?

According to Michigan's Administrative Rules to the Occupational Code, after a sales agreement has been fully executed, a licensee is not required to submit additional offers to the seller. Based on the fact that the fiduciary duties do not terminate until after the closing, a seller that is bound to an accepted offer may wish to view a later offer as a possible backup or secondary offer. If the seller wishes to continue to see additional offers, the seller must reserve the right in his or her service provision agreement. Some Michigan brokers have chosen to include a statement in their service provision specifying whether or not the licensee is required to present these additional offers. Other service provision agreements give the seller a choice of the two.

4.C.4   Once the offer is accepted, what rights does the buyer have in the property?

After a purchase agreement is signed, and the buyer or buyer's agent is in receipt of the signed document, equitable title passes to the purchaser. The seller cannot arbitrarily withdraw his acceptance and sell to another party.

4.C.5   What is meant by "dual contracts" and why are they illegal in Michigan?

Dual contracts refer to two contracts from the same buyer on the same property. One of the offers is used **to purchase** the property while the other is used **to finance** the property. The offer to purchase can be either written or oral, while the offer to finance is generally written.

The true purchase price is known only between the contracting parties. The purpose of these contracts is to enable the buyer *to obtain a larger loan* than the true sale price or to enable the buyer to *qualify for a loan* that the buyer otherwise could not obtain. Thus, the lender is deceived. In Michigan, any persons, including the buyer and seller, who engage in this practice are guilty of a fraud and can be criminally prosecuted for a conspiracy to defraud a regulated lender. This fraudulent practice also violates the Department's rules in that a licensee has a duty to make certain that all terms and conditions of sale are included in the offer to purchase.

4.C.6 What duties does the licensee have after the contract is signed?

A licensee must deliver a signed copy of the offer to the buyer immediately upon its execution. Upon obtaining acceptance of the offer (seller's signature), the licensee must deliver true, executed copies to the buyer and seller.

Acceptable methods of contract delivery include in person, by mail, or electronic communication. In order to use electronic records or digital signatures in a real estate transaction, the parties must give prior approval. Electronic communications are regulated by the Uniform Electronic Transfers Act (PA 305 of 2000).

D. CLOSINGS

4.D.1 Who is responsible for the accuracy of a closing?

The listing broker is responsible for the closing even though the task may be delegated to another entity or a cooperating broker. Therefore, Michigan law authorizes the listing company to call the shots. A broker must close a transaction according to the terms of the buyer's and seller's written agreement. If the written agreement does not make sense, or if the transaction has changed, the broker must obtain buyer and seller written approval before modifying the transaction.

A salesperson may prepare closing statements and conduct closings under the broker's direct supervision. Regardless of who is conducting the closing, the broker must sign the final closing statement.

4.D.2 Who is responsible for providing copies of all of these documents and for how long must they be kept on file?

Detailed closing statements must be provided to the buyer and seller. The statement must show the receipts and disbursements affecting that party. The broker or associate broker must sign the statements and is responsible for their content.

Michigan law does not specify a time requirement regarding the executed contracts. However, all trust account records must be maintained for three years.

4.D.3 Can brokers charge to prepare some documents?

A broker can only prepare documents for a transaction in which he or she was involved as an agent or transactional coordinator. Otherwise, he or she will be engaging in the unauthorized practice of law.

E.   STIGMATIZED PROPERTIES

4.E.1 What is a stigmatized property?

A stigmatized property is one that has acquired an undesirable reputation. Stigmatized properties include homes with recorded paranormal activities, those psychologically impacted by newsworthy incidents like murder or murder/suicide, or those suspected of being a front for illegal drug sales or a site of a forcible felony.

4.E.2 Is there any responsibility for failure to disclose information about stigmatized property?

The essence of the issue is discovery, not disclosure. There is no duty for the seller to disclose information regarding stigmatized property that has no material effect on the condition of the property.

Based on the Michigan Occupational Code, no cause of action is warranted against a buyer's agent for failure to discover that the purchased property was psychologically impacted. This means that the Department will not discipline a licensee for nondisclosure.

However, it could be argued that if the buyer's agent had prior knowledge, then under agency law, the buyer's agent may have a duty to disclose the known information. A civil suit for breach of fiduciary duty is separate from a complaint filed with the Department. The courts are not required to follow the regulations found in the Occupational Code in a private suit between an agent and a principal. To date, there are no reported Michigan cases that have created this duty on the agent.

4.E.3   Are there any other disclosure or non disclosures required in Michigan?

Similarly, a licensee is not required to disclose information that is available under the Sex Offenders Registration Act. Under the Americans with Disabilities Act, the federal fair housing laws, and Michigan's Persons with Disabilities Act, a licensee is *prohibited* from disclosing any information regarding a former occupant's disability, or in particular, that the seller has HIV or AIDS. The Occupational Code reinforces this by stating that failure to disclose this information is not a violation of the law.

F.   ENVIRONMENTAL CONCERNS

4.F.1   Who implements CERCLA in Michigan?

The Natural Resources and Environmental Protection Act is Michigan's version of CERCLA. The federal Environmental Protection Agency identifies polluted sites and creates a National Priorities List (NPL) for cleanup.

The Michigan Department of Environmental Quality (MDEQ) administers programs involving cleanup and redevelopment. The MDEQ, through its Environmental Response Division, manages the federal Superfund program. In Michigan, private parties may sue in state or federal court.

4.F.2   Who is responsible for cleaning up hazardous waste on a property?

The MDEQ will attempt to identify liable parties and assist them in remediation. It will attempt to resolve cleanup and cost recovery issues through voluntary actions. When necessary, the MDEQ can compel compliance through civil actions. To avoid future environmental liability for a preexisting condition, a buyer should obtain a baseline environmental assessment.

4.F.3   What are wetlands, and where may a buyer go to learn more about wetlands protection?

A wetland is land characterized by the presence of water at a frequency and duration sufficient to support, and that under normal circumstances does support, wetland vegetation or aquatic life and is commonly referred to as a *bog, swamp,* or *marsh.* The regulations apply to wetlands that are contiguous to the Great Lakes or Lake St. Clair, an inland lake or pond, or a river or stream.

Wetlands that are not contiguous, but are more than five acres in size and are in a county of less than 100,000 population are regulated only if the MDEQ has completed its inventory in the county. Wetlands that are not contiguous and are five acres or less in size may be regulated where the MDEQ has notified the owner that the protection of the area is essential to the preservation of the natural resources of the state from pollution, impairment, or destruction.

In 1995, the Goemare-Anderson Wetland Protection Act became part of the Natural Resource and Environmental Protection Act. In order to preserve and protect Michigan wetlands, the MDEQ is authorized to regulate uses and issue permits. It also establishes guidelines for local wetland regulation.

4.F.4   What activities are regulated and which are allowed?

The following activities require a permit from the MDEQ:

- Depositing fill material in a wetland
- Dredging or removing of soil or minerals from a wetland
- Constructing or operating a development in a wetland
- Draining surface water

Maintenance of roads in a right-of-way, power lines, and gas or oil pipelines must be performed in a manner that minimizes any adverse effect on the wetland. The operation and maintenance of serviceable structures and dikes or levees in existence on October 1, 1980, are allowed.

Recreational uses such as fishing, trapping, hunting, swimming, boating, and hiking are allowed. Likewise, agricultural uses are also permissible, such as grazing of animals, farming, horticulture, silviculture, lumbering, and ranching activities, including plowing, irrigation, irrigation ditching, seeding, cultivating, minor drainage, harvesting for the production of food, fiber, and forest products, or upland soil and water conservation practices.

4.F.5   What are the civil and criminal penalties for violating the Wetland Protection Act?

When a person violates a condition of a permit, the MDEQ will issue an order requiring compliance. If the violator does not comply within the stated time period, the Attorney General may bring a civil action or obtain an injunction.

In addition to any other remedies, the court may impose a civil fine of not more than $10,000 per day of violation. Additionally, the court may order a person who violates this part to restore, as nearly as possible, the wetland that was affected by the violation to its original condition, including the removal of fill material deposited or the replacement of soil, sand, or minerals.

A person who willfully or recklessly violates a condition, or a corporate officer who has knowledge of or is responsible for a violation, is guilty of a misdemeanor. This misdemeanor is punishable by a fine of up to $2,500, but no more than $25,000 per day of violation, and/or imprisonment for up to one year. A second or subsequent violation is a felony, punishable by a fine of up to $50,000 for each day of violation and/or imprisonment for up to two years.

4.F.6   Are there other laws and/or state agencies that control rights to water in Michigan?

Michigan has over 38,000 miles of streams and more than 11,000 lakes and ponds, making water one of Michigan's primary environmental concerns. Some of the laws affecting water rights include the following:

- **Part 305 of the Natural Resources and Environmental Protection Act** (previously the Natural River Act of 1970) regulates a system of designated wild scenic and recreational rivers and protects the designated river frontage.
- **Part 323 of the Natural Resources and Environmental Protection Act** (previously the Shorelands Protection and Management Act of 1970) authorizes the Water Resources Commission to protect and manage shorelands in close proximity to any of the Great Lakes or a connecting waterway.
- **Part 32 of the Natural Resources and Environmental Protection Act** (previously the Great Lakes Preservation Act) prevents diversion of Great Lakes water within the Michigan borders to an area outside of the Great Lakes basin.
- **Part 353 of the Natural Resources and Environmental Protection Act** (previously the Sand Dune Protection and Management Act) regulates activities within designated critical dune areas.
- **The Soil Erosion and Sedimentation Control Act of 1972** teams the Water Resources Commission with the Department of Agriculture to control soil erosion and sedimentation. The act requires a permit to disturb one or more acres of land within 500 feet of stream or lake.
- **Water Resources Commission Act** regulates discharge of water and content of discharge.

4.F.7   Are there other water-related issues?

Customarily, well testing is done in Michigan for bacteria and high levels of nitrate. The residential property seller disclosure statement should include copies of water tests, if available. The Michigan Department of Public Health is the definitive authority over water quality.

4.F.8   Of what should the buyer be aware before building on an acreage and installing a septic system?

In Michigan, county health officials monitor septic tanks and private sewage disposal systems. Michigan allows the use of both aerobic and anaerobic systems. For proper drainage, the ground must be able to absorb the liquid waste. A percolation test is conducted which monitors the time that it takes water poured through a pipe to be absorbed by the soil. A permit may not be issued if there is insufficient absorption.

4.F.9   Are there other issues of which a developer should be aware?

Although not environmental issues, the Right to Farm Act and the Land Division Act are important to buyers that are purchasing for the purpose of development. Both of these will be discussed in Chapter 7.

4.F.10   Does Michigan have a Lead-Based Paint Hazard Reduction Law?

Michigan operates under the federal Residential Lead-Based Paint Hazard Reduction Act of 1992 and Title X, Lead-Based Paint Poisoning Prevention Act. This legislation requires sellers, landlords, and their agents to provide prior to the sale or lease of the property information regarding the health hazards resulting from the possible exposure of lead-based paint in all pre-1978 residential and apartment dwellings. It also gives the a buyer the right of a 10-day inspection to determine whether the property does or does not have lead-based paint.

The Michigan Department of Community Health is the authority on lead-based paint issues. In Michigan, the EPA has jurisdiction over lead-based paint disclosure enforcement. Michigan has also adopted and administers the Lead Abatement Act, which establishes accreditation of training, certification of individuals, and work practice standards for lead-based paint activities

4.F.11   Does Michigan require any other disclosures of environmental presence, such as asbestos, UFFI, etc.?

No other specific disclosures are required, except those that are required in the Sellers Disclosure Statement. The seller must answer the following question: "Are you [seller] aware of any substances, materials or products that may be an environmental hazard such as, but not limited to, asbestos, radon gas, formaldehyde, lead-based paint, fuel or chemical storage tanks, and contaminated spoil on the property?"

4.F.12 Are there any other environmental issue of which to be aware?

Underground storage tanks must be disclosed on the Sellers Disclosure Statement. Underground storage tanks used for regulated substances must be registered with the MDEQ. Farm or residential tanks, tanks of 1,100 gallons or less used for storing motor fuel or heating oil, and septic tanks are specifically excluded from the regulation.

4.F.13 What is the Michigan Environmental Protection Act (MEPA)?

The MEPA fulfills Michigan's constitutional mandate that legislatures pass laws to promote the public health and to protect the air, water, and other natural resources. A private person, or any government or legal entity, may bring an action or may intervene in administrative proceedings that may have the effect of significantly impacting the environment. MEPA allows private parties to curtail the rights of property owners when the owner's actions are likely to have an adverse effect on the environment.

4.F.14 What activities are regulated and which are allowed?

Activities that significantly impact the air, water, or other natural resources may be limited or prohibited. A court may take action if pollution, impairment, or destruction exists, or is likely. An activity will be allowed if the defendant can show there is no feasible and prudent alternative to his conduct and that the conduct is consistent with the promotion of the public health, safety, and welfare.

4.F.15 What are the civil and criminal penalties allowed under MEPA?

The act provides for declaratory and equitable relief, such as a temporary or permanent injunction, or a declaration of acceptable levels of discharge of pollutants. A party cannot obtain monetary damages or recover attorney fees. There are no criminal penalties provided.

G. ABSTRACTING

4.G.1 Is Michigan a title or lien theory state?

Michigan is a lien theory state. A mortgage acts as a lien against the real estate, it does not convey title. Liens must be foreclosed before title can transfer. In order to foreclose a lien, including a mortgage, through nonjudicial foreclosure, the document must contain a nonjudicial power of sale. State statutes authorize the use of a power of sale. Nonjudicial foreclosure is also referred to as *statutory foreclosure*, or *foreclosure by advertisement*.

4.G.2   How does a buyer know that title to the property is "good and marketable?"

A licensee who is working with a buyer at the time of the offer to purchase must recommend to the buyer that the buyer request that the seller provide him with a fee title insurance policy in the amount of the purchase price. The title policy is to be certified to the date of closing. This request is usually preprinted into the offer to purchase.

Prior to the closing, the insurance company will search the public records and issue a title insurance commitment showing liens and encumbrances currently on the property. It is the buyer's responsibility to examine the commitment and determine whether the title is marketable.

4.G.3   Which party is responsible for searching public records?

Although the buyer has asked the seller to purchase the fee title insurance policy on his behalf, and the title insurer is doing the title search, it is ultimately up to buyers to protect their own interests.

4.G.4   What is the difference between marketable and insurable title?

No title is completely clear or free of defects. A marketable title is reasonably free from defects, so that a court would compel a purchaser to complete the transaction. An insurable title is one for which a title insurance company will cover the risk of the defects, so that if a claim is made the insurance company will defend the buyer's claim up to the price of the policy.

Most preprinted offers to purchase require that the seller provide insurable title. A title that is not marketable is often insurable if a title insurance company is willing to take the risk of the encumbrance unless the encumbrance was excluded from the coverage. This means that the buyer may lose his property to the encumbrance, but that the insurance company will have to reimburse him for his monetary loss, but only up to the amount of the policy, typically, the purchase price of the house. The buyer may still face the aggravation of moving and finding a new place to live and he will lose any appreciation that may have occurred in the market value.

4.G.5   What is the mortgagee's title insurance policy?

When a mortgage loan is obtained, the lender will require that the borrower provide it with a mortgagee's title insurance policy in the amount of the loan principal. This policy will pay off the borrower's loan if the property is lost to a title defect.

The mortgagee's and fee title polices are typically ordered at the same time. This allows the mortgagee's policy to be discounted in price since only one search needs to be performed. This is called a *simultaneous issue*. The insurance commission requires each insurance company to post its premiums and to charge everyone the same premium for the same service.

4.G.6   What is the 40-year Marketable Title Act?

The 40-year Marketable Title Act is a statute of limitations. A title search only needs to show an unbroken chain of title going back 40 years. A court is not allowed to hear most claims that are older than 40 years.

H.   CONVEYANCE TAXES

4.H.1   What are conveyance taxes?

For increased revenue, Michigan charges property owners a transfer tax when they transfer legal title to their properties. Historically, Michigan used differing denomination stamps (postage size) to record the amount of the tax and affixed them to the deed. The stamps were then franked (defaced) to show that the tax had been paid.

To the property owner, it was considered a transfer tax stamp. To the state of Michigan, it was considered a revenue stamp. To the recorder's office, it was considered a documentary stamp. In reality, it was the same thing looked at from three perspectives, and the terminology is interchanged.

Today, Michigan just uses a receipt and affixes it to the deed for recordation. However, it is still referred to as a revenue stamp, but it is not—it is a revenue tax

4.H.2   How are conveyances taxes computed?

Michigan has two transfer taxes: the state tax and the county tax. Transfer tax is paid on the value of real estate being transferred upon transfer of the deed. County transfer tax is paid at the rate of $0.55 for each $500, or fraction thereof. In other words, any portion of $500 will be rounded up to the next $500, e.g., $510 is taxed as $1,000. State transfer tax is paid at the rate of $3.75 for each $500, or fraction thereof.

For example, here is how to compute the taxes on a $210,700 sale. $210,700 divided by $500 = 421.4 rounded up to 422 times $.55 = $232.10 county tax. The state tax is 422 times $3.75 = $1,582.50.

4.H.3　Who is responsible for paying these taxes?

The seller or grantor is required to pay the transfer tax, unless the parties agree otherwise. The tax is collected at the time that the deed is recorded, by which time the seller may be long gone. A prudent buyer or buyer's agent will have the transfer tax deducted from the seller's final proceeds and credited to the buyer.

License Law Enforcement Overview

This chapter covers how the Michigan Department of Real Estate Consumer and Industry Services considers violations of license law or rule. Generally, after proper disciplinary hearings, the Department exercises its control over licensees through public reprimands, reeducation, fines, and the denial, suspension, or revocation of licenses. The director is the executive head of the Department.

A. LICENSE LAW ENFORCEMENT

5.A.1 Is a violation of Michigan license law a misdemeanor or a felony?

Most violations under Michigan license law are considered simple misdemeanors. The Department may refer a complaint against a nonlicensee to any court of competent jurisdiction and take any necessary legal actions to enforce the law and collect penalties.

5.A.2 Under what circumstances may the Michigan Real Estate Commission investigate licensees?

The Department investigates all complaints that allege a violation of the licensing act, a rule, or order. Any affected person, including a member of the public, a private association, the Department, the Board, or the attorney general's office, may file a complaint.

5.A.3 What are some of the violations for which a complaint can be filed?

The Department is charged with protecting the interests of the public. Consequently, the Department has jurisdiction over actions by a licensee that can harm the consumer in a real estate transaction.

The Department must investigate each complaint. If the investigative unit (see 5.A.5) does not find evidence of a violation, the complaint will be closed. A complaint is a grievance; this is different from a formal complaint, which is a list of alleged violations.

A complaint can be filed against a person who practices fraud, deceit, or dishonesty in obtaining a license or practicing the real estate occupation and/or who

- violates a rule of conduct;
- demonstrates a lack of good moral character (fair, open, honest);
- commits gross negligence;
- engages in false advertising;
- exhibits incompetence;
- refuses to respond to a citation;
- fails to comply with a subpoena or final order; or
- violates any other provision of the Occupational Code or its rules.

It is also a violation to represent more than one party in a transaction without full knowledge of the parties (except in a property management transaction). Examples of other violations:

- Failing to provide the required written agency disclosure statement
- Representing a broker other than the employer without the employing broker's knowledge and consent
- Changing a business location without notifying the department
- Paying a fee to an unlicensed person
- Failing to properly maintain property management accounts
- Charging for a market analysis without disclosing that it was produced by a real estate licensee, not by a licensed appraiser
- A broker's failure to return a salesperson or associate broker's license within five days of the written notice of termination of employment

5.A.4 Under what conditions may a broker pay a fee to an unlicensed person?

In order to collect a commission or other compensation for performing real estate activities, a person must prove that he or she was licensed at the time the activity occurred. Similarly, it is a violation for a licensee to share a commission with another person that is not licensed, but there are several exceptions.

A licensee may purchase a commercially prepared list of names. A broker can pay a broker who is licensed in another state as long as the out-of-state broker does not conduct in this state a negotiation for which a commission is paid. An owner or his agent may pay an existing tenant up to one-half month's rent for the referral fee of a new tenant.

5.A.5   How does the Department determine when and if to follow up on a complaint?

The investigative unit of the Department conducts investigations. If there is evidence of a violation, the Department or the attorney general's office may issue a formal complaint, a cease and desist order, a summary suspension, or a citation. A summary suspension, a cease and desist order, or an injunction is in addition to any action taken against the license or licensee, such as criminal prosecution or a formal complaint. If the investigative unit cannot complete the investigation within 30 days, it must provide a status report to the director.

5.A.6   Under what circumstances may the investigative unit decide not to hold a hearing?

If the investigative unit determines that there was no probable cause that warrants discipline, a letter is sent, and the case closed. If the respondent is in current compliance, or if the parties settle the matter to the Department's satisfaction, a hearing will not be held.

Recall that the mission of the Department is to protect the public. Thus, Department rules do not authorize the Department to consider or conduct hearings involving disputes over fees or commissions between cooperating brokers, salespersons, and other brokers.

5.A.7   How does the Commission decide on holding a hearing?

A hearing will be the ultimate outcome of all legitimate, unresolved complaints.

5.A.8   What are the remedies to a violation?

A person, school, or institution that violates the Occupational Code or an administrative rule is subject to one or more of the following remedies:

- A limitation on a license
- Suspension, revocation, or denial of a license or its renewal

- Censure
- Probation
- Restitution
- Civil fine of up to $10,000

Where restitution is required, the license may be suspended until the restitution is completed. A party may also bring a civil suit for any alleged violations.

5.A.9   What is meant by a limitation on a license?

A limitation is a condition or restriction placed on a license, including any of the following limitations:

- Only specified functions may be performed.
- Activities may only be performed for a specified period of time or within a certain geographical area.
- Restitution must be made or certain work performed.
- Financial statements certified by a CPA. must be filed at regular intervals.
- An attorney must review all contracts.
- The licensee must file a surety bond.
- Money must be deposited in an escrow account for disbursement under certain conditions.
- The licensee must file reports with the Department at predetermined intervals.
- Any other requirement that assures the licensee's competence

5.A.10   What is a cease and desist order?

After an investigation, the Director may issue a cease and desist order. The person against whom the order is issued has **30 days** to file a written request for a hearing. A violation of the cease and desist order may result in the attorney general seeking an injunction to prevent the person from violating the order. An injunction is essentially an order to stop something, such as stop stealing from the escrow account or stop discriminating.

5.A.11   What is a summary suspension?

After an investigation, the Department, upon belief in an imminent threat to the public health, safety, or welfare, may issue a summary (immediate) suspension. Upon receipt of a petition to dissolve the order, the Department must immediately schedule a hearing on the suspension.

At the hearing, the Department must bring sufficient evidence of threat to the public health, safety, or welfare, requiring emergency action, in order to continue the suspension order. The hearing record of the summary suspension will become part of the record on the complaint in any subsequent hearing.

5.A.12   Can the Department request an informal conference?

During the investigation, or after a formal complaint is issued, the Department may attempt to bring the parties together at an informal conference in order to attempt to settle the matter. A board or committee member may attend an informal conference.

The informal conference may result in a settlement, including a consent order, waiver, default, censure, probation, restitution, penalty, or the revocation, suspension, or limitation of a license. If an informal conference does not result in a settlement, the matter will go to a hearing.

5.A.13   What happens if a formal complaint is filed?

A formal complaint is a list of the alleged charges issued after the complaint (not formal) has been investigated and the Department has evidence indicating that a violation may have occurred. The formal complaint is served on the respondent with a notice describing the conference and hearing processes.

The respondent has 15 days in which to choose to negotiate a settlement, show compliance, or proceed to a contested case hearing. If the respondent does not choose one of the three options within the 15 days, the Department will automatically proceed to the hearing.

5.A.14   What is the effect of a citation?

The best analogy for a citation is a traffic ticket—a notice of violation is issued and a fine is paid. A citation may be mailed or issued in person. It will contain the date, issuing person's name and title, respondent's name and address, and a brief description of the alleged violation. It will also list actions required for compliance and a fine of up to $100 per violation. The respondent must sign a receipt of the citation, but this signature is not an admission of guilt.

The respondent has 30 days to agree to accept the terms of the citation and notify the Department. If the respondent admits to the violation, he or she may also submit a one-page explanation to be included in his file. An admission to a citation has the same effect as a final order and can be disclosed to the public. The citation will be removed from the records if the respondent does not have any additional disciplinary actions within the next five years.

If the respondent refuses to admit to the violation alleged in the citation within 30 days of receipt, then the citation will become a formal complaint and that process will begin. Incidentally, to date, the Department has never issued a citation for a real estate matter.

5.A.15   How is a hearing held?

A hearing, at times referred to as a *contested case hearing,* is similar to a trial. An administrative law hearings examiner will preside and the Department and the respondent will each be entitled to present their case. The Department is represented by one of its employees and the respondent may bring counsel. A circuit court may issue an order compelling a person to testify or produce evidence at an informal conference or hearing.

After the hearing, the administrative law hearings examiner will produce a hearing report containing fact findings and legal conclusions. A copy will be sent to the Department, the attorney general, the Board, the complainant, and the respondent. The report will recommend penalties.

5.A.16   What are the legal effects of the Hearing and possible disciplinary actions?

Upon receiving a hearing report, the Board has 60 days to assess a penalty (see 5.A.8) or issue a limitation (see 5.A.9). As an aid, the Board may request a transcript of the hearing. If the transcript has been requested, the time period is extended to 60 days from receipt of the transcript. If the Board cannot assess a penalty within these time periods, then the director may assess the penalty and issue a final order. A board member who has participated in the investigation or attended an informal conference may not participate in the final resolution of the complaint.

Additionally, a person or school may be enjoined from practicing without a license and the complainant may recover actual costs and attorney fees. The Department may criminally prosecute violations and the attorney general may intervene in and prosecute the case.

If a licensee has been disciplined in the past, the Department may require that the licensee post a surety bond as a condition to licensure. The bond may not exceed the sum of $5,000 or the period of five years. A person who is subsequently harmed by the licensee may then make a claim for damages against the bond.

5.A.17   What are the criminal penalties for violation of the law?

Violation of the Occupational Code is a criminal misdemeanor and may be prosecuted in a court of law. The criminal prosecution is separate from the Department's hearing process and disciplinary action. Only a court of law, not a state agency such as the Department, may issue a criminal penalty or send a person to jail.

The first offense is punishable by a fine of up to $500 and/or imprisonment for up to 90 days. A second or subsequent offense is punishable by a fine of up to $1,000 and/or imprisonment of up to one year.

5.A.18   What happens if the respondent does not appear at the hearing?

The hearing will be held without the licensee. The licensee will be bound by the decision as if the licensee had been there. In other words, the licensee loses the right to cross-examine witnesses and to present the licensee's defense.

5.A.19   Is there any possibility of an appeal from a hearing?

The Code does not address appeal from a hearing, per se. However, a person may file a petition.

A person who does not receive a license or renewal may petition the Department and the Board for review. The petition must be in writing and specify the reasons that the license should be issued. In considering a petition, the Department and the Board may administer an alternate form of testing or conduct a personal interview. Upon considering a petition, the Department and the Board may determine that the person can perform with competence and issue the license or renewal.

Where a limitation has been placed on a license, a person has 30 days to file a written petition for review. The Department then has 15 days to respond with its reasons for placing the limitation. The Department and the Board may remove the limitation if they determine that the person can perform with competence.

B.   SUSPENDED OR REVOKED LICENSES

5.B.1   What are the immediate effects of a suspended or revoked designated broker's license?

A suspended or revoked license must be returned to the Department, and as of the effective date, the right to engage in activities that require a license is terminated. The revocation of the broker (brokerage) license, or sole associate broker license, thereby disabling the broker license, automatically places on suspended status every license held by the broker by virtue of their employment. These licensees may return to real estate activities only when transferred to another broker.

5.B.2   What are the effects on brokerage agreements when the designated broker's license is suspended or revoked?

Upon receipt of the Department's order, property management agreements and service provision agreements, that is, listing and buyer brokerage agreements, are automatically canceled. Sellers and lessors must be apprised of their rights to list or lease with someone else. It is illegal to sell or assign listings or management agreements without written authorization of the seller or lessor.

5.B.3   Is the designated broker disciplined if one of his or her licensees is disciplined?

Any unlawful act or violation by a licensee is not cause for the revocation of the broker's license unless the broker had guilty knowledge of the unlawful act or violation. The broker or associate broker is responsible for supervising his or her licensees. It is possible that an inadequately supervised licensee may cause the broker to be in violation of his duty to supervise.

5.B.4   Who is responsible for proving misconduct?

The Department bears the burden of proof in regard to all allegations and cannot assume facts that are not in evidence or compel a party to prove his or her innocence.

C.   ERRORS AND OMISSIONS INSURANCE OR RECOVERY FUND

5.C.1   Does Michigan have a recovery fund for victims?

Michigan does not have a state recovery fund available for real estate consumers who have been damaged by a real estate licensee. It has, however, created a Construction Lien Recovery Fund for victims of unscrupulous builders who have paid for construction but are in jeopardy of having a lien foreclosed because of alleged nonpayment. This topic is explored further in section 7.B.2.

5.C.2   Are Michigan licensees required to obtain bonding or Errors and Omissions Insurance?

Michigan law does not require licensees to be bonded unless the Department has required that a licensee carry the bond.

5.C.3   What is Errors and Omissions (E & O) Insurance?

Licensees may purchase errors and omissions insurance to protect themselves against any oversights that they may have committed in their professional capacity. The coverage extends to inadvertent errors but will not protect against intentional acts or fraud. Fair housing violations are specifically excluded from coverage. Michigan does not require that licensees carry this insurance.

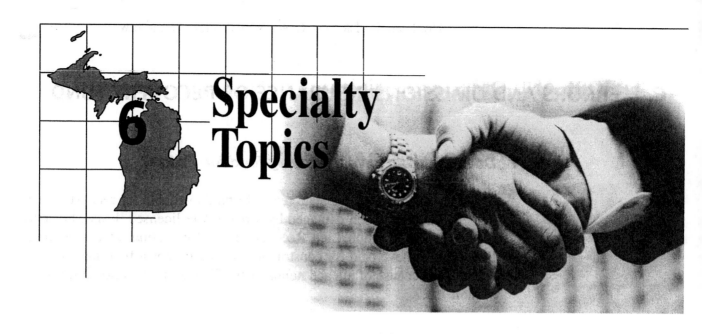

6 Specialty Topics

M any other professions and issues touch real estate brokerage. This chapter discusses appraisal requirements, landlord-tenant activities, and forms of ownership recognized in Michigan. Numerous laws relating to borrowing money are also included.

A. RELATED REAL ESTATE ACTIVITIES

6.A.1 What are Michigan state requirements for appraisers?

Under Article 26 of the Occupational Code, appraisers are required to obtain a license.

6.A.2 What are the various designations and what may each appraise?

The various appraisal designations depend upon education and experience.

- *Limited real estate appraiser* (previously known as *valuation specialist*) may appraise property for nonfederally related transactions.
- *Licensed real estate appraiser* may appraise property involving non-federally related transactions; all types of property with values up to $250,000; and federally related loans, 1-family to 4-family residential property with values up to $1,000,000.
- *Certified residential real estate appraiser* may appraise federally related transactions involving residential property of any value and nonresidential properties of up to $250,000 in value.
- *Certified general real estate appraiser* may appraise any type property of any value.

A licensed appraiser who is not licensed to appraise a certain type of property may always assist an authorized appraiser. His or her contribution must be noted, and he or she cannot sign the report.

6.A.3   How many hours of education must each candidate complete and what experience is required?

The *limited* real estate appraiser must complete 75 hours, including 15 hours of the Uniform Standards of Professional Appraisal Practice (USPAP); no experience is required. The *licensed* real estate appraiser must complete a total of 90 hours, including 15 hours of USPAP, and complete 2,000 hours of appraising, of which a minimum of 1,500 hours are residential appraisals.

The *certified residential* real estate appraiser must complete classroom courses of 120 hours, including 15 hours of USPAP. The certified appraiser must have completed 2,500 hours of appraising, of which at least 2,000 are residential. Finally, the *certified general* real estate appraiser must complete180 hours, including 90 hours of nonresidential courses and 15 hours of USPAP. The certified candidate must have completed at least 3,000 hours of appraisals of which 1,500 must be on nonresidential properties.

All appraisers, other than the limited real estate appraiser, are required to pass an examination.

6.A.4   Are appraisers required to take continuing education courses?

Yes, the limited real estate appraiser must take at least 14 hours of CE per year after the second renewal. All other appraisers must complete 28 hours every two years after the first renewal.

6.A.5   Do home inspectors have to be licensed?

At the present time, there is no requirement for licensing of home inspectors.

B.   FORMS OF OWNERSHIP

6.B.1   What forms of ownership are recognized in Michigan?

Michigan recognizes ownership in severalty (individual), tenancy in common, joint tenancy, and tenancy by the entireties.

In regard to joint tenancy, Michigan case law makes a distinction between the language *joint tenants* and *joint tenants with full rights of survivorship,* or similar survivorship language. Joint tenants with full rights of survivorship has the same characteristics as joint tenancy but may not be severed by conveyance. A conveyance by one of the tenants with full rights of survivorship will give the grantee and the remaining cotenants joint life estates with dual contingent remainders. The measuring lives remain those of the original cotenants, not the life span of the new grantee.

6.B.2   Are dower and curtesy recognized in Michigan?

Michigan does not acknowledge curtesy. The common-law concept of dower has been codified into the Michigan Revised Probate Code. Dower is a life estate in one-third of the husband's real estate that was owned in severalty or in common.

Dower rights are seldom exercised because the Probate Code allows the surviving spouse the option to take under the will, to take a statutory share, or if a widow, to take dower. The statutory share is one-half of what the spouse would have obtained had the decedent died without a will, reduced by one-half of the value of all property transferring to the spouse outside of the probate proceedings, which is usually more generous than dower.

6.B.3   Can married couples designate separate and community property?

Michigan is not a community property state.

C.   OTHER FORMS OF PROPERTY OWNERSHIP

6.C.1   What about partnerships, corporations, etc.?

The Michigan Uniform Partnership Act governs partnership interests. All partners must join in a conveyance of the partnership property. The interest of each individual partner is inseparable from the partnership itself and cannot be conveyed separately from the partnership interest. Similarly, only creditors of the partnership may attach a partnership interest. Death of a partner vests ownership in the surviving partners for the purpose of dissolution.

A corporation is an artificial entity separate from its owners. Title is held by the corporation and controlled by the board of directors and shareholders.

6.C.2   What are timeshares? Do they have to be registered?

Timeshares are a form of ownership interest that allows for the use of a property for a fixed or variable period of time, but not less than a full year. The Condominium Act provides for timeshare interests over a period of at least five years. Anyone selling timeshares must hold a broker's license.

6.C.3   Under what circumstances may a timeshare purchaser rescind his or her contract?

There is a cooling off period under the provisions of the Condominium Act. A purchaser of a newly constructed condominium, including a timeshare or a conversion unit, has nine days from the receipt of the required condominium documents, or from the time he or she signed the purchase agreement, whichever occurs last, to rescind the purchase agreement.

A condominium buyer can withdraw within nine days for any, or no, reason. A reservation agreement, as opposed to a purchase agreement, can be canceled at any time, and all payments must be refunded within three days.

6.C.4   What is the difference between a condo and a cooperative?

In a *cooperative,* the occupants hold shares in the organization that owns the real estate. A not-for-profit corporation is the most common type of ownership organization. By purchasing shares in the cooperative corporation, the purchaser becomes an owner-tenant. The real estate is taxed in the name of the cooperative, but the individual owner-tenants are allowed to take tax deductions for the individual amounts paid as well as the same homestead tax credit and exemption as afforded individual property owners.

In *condominium* ownership, each unit is individually owned and the individual dwelling owner is individually taxed. The Michigan Condominium Act covers condominium housing. It is important to remember that condominium is a form of ownership, not a style of building, and that townhouse is a style of building, not a form of ownership. Condo ownership is not limited to residential units; office buildings and other commercial real estate can also be condominium owned. The condo law applies to residential units, marina units (dockominiums), mobile home units, timeshares, and site condominiums (building envelope).

6.C.5   What Michigan laws govern cooperative and condominium ownership?

Several laws govern multiple housing:

- Cooperative corporations, MCLA 450.98–.109, MSA 21.99–.110
- Michigan Nonprofit Corporations Act, MCLA 450.2101 et seq., MSA 21.197(101) et seq.
- Michigan Uniform Securities Act, MCLA 451.501 et seq., MSA 19.776(101). Securities Act of 1933, 15 USC 77a et seq.
- Condominium Act, MCLA 559.101 et seq., MSA 26.50(101) et seq.

6.C.6   What are association dues and how are unpaid dues collected?

Association dues are sums assessed by the council of co-owners in order to pay for the maintenance of the common areas and other association costs. Unpaid association dues for the share of the common expenses chargeable to any unit constitute a lien and can be foreclosed on by suit from the council of co-owners or the association management company representing the co-owners. In other words, as a form of protest, nonpayment of association dues is not a good idea.

6.C.7   Are cooperatives required to be registered?

Cooperatives may resemble investment securities and must be registered unless an exemption is available. They are usually exempt from registration under the federal Securities Act of 1933, since there is no profit motive. However, this does not necessarily hold true under Michigan law.

The Michigan Corporations and Securities Bureau takes the position that, generally, shares in a cooperative apartment project must be registered. An exemption order will be issued if: (1) the project is under the supervisory control of a state or federal government agency; (2) all construction and improvements will be completed before any shares are sold; and (3) the purchaser receives disclosure of all material information (same as a condo project).

6.C.8   What documents must be given to condo buyers?

The buyer must be given a copy of the purchase agreement, copy of the recorded master deed, including bylaws, the *Condominium Buyer's Handbook,* and a disclosure statement. The master deed provides percentages of value for the individual units. The bylaws govern the administration of the project and the voting rights in the association. The bylaws are recorded together with the master deed.

The *Condominium Buyer's Handbook* is a state-authorized pamphlet explaining the condominium concept. The disclosure statement includes information regarding matters such as the association's possible liability; name, address, and experience of each developer and management company; projected budget; explanation of escrow arrangement; warranties, or lack thereof; and if a conversion condominium, the condition of the building components.

6.C.9   Do existing tenants have any rights during the conversion from rental to condo?

A tenant in a rental apartment that is being converted to a condominium may stay in the unit for 120 days from receipt of the notice, or to the end of the lease, whichever is longer. A tenant may terminate an existing lease upon a 60-day notice. A person who is 65 years of age or older or who is paraplegic, quadriplegic, hemiplegic, or blind must be allowed to continue to lease, depending on the circumstances, for a period of one to ten years.

6.C.10   Under what conditions may condo owners rent out their units?

A unit co-owner has the right to rent his or her unit, unless it is prohibited by the condominium documents. A co-owner, including the developer, who intends to rent the unit for more than 30 days must provide the association with

- a copy of the proposed lease prior to the rental,
- a copy of the executed lease after the rental, and
- the name of all of the occupants.

If a tenant breaches any of the conditions in the condominium documents and the co-owner does not correct the breach, the association may bring a summary proceeding action for eviction against the tenant and, simultaneously, for money damages against the co-owner and tenant. The association may notify a tenant of a co-owner's arrearage, allowing the tenant to pay the arrearage and future assessments and to deduct them from the rent owed.

6.C.11   May a condo unit owner make modifications to his or her condo unit?

A co-owner may make modifications to his or her unit. Such modifications may include modifications to common elements and to the route from the public way to the door, in order to facilitate access to or movement within the unit, or to alleviate conditions that could be hazardous for persons with disabilities who reside in or regularly visit the unit. The modification is to be made at the co-owner's expense.

A co-owner who has made exterior modifications must provide written notification to the association of his or her intent to sell or lease the unit at least 30 days before the transfer. The association then has 30 days to require the co-owner to remove the modification at his or her own expense. However, the association may not require the removal of a modification if the co-owner intends to resume residing in the unit within 12 months or if he or she transfers the unit to a person with disabilities who needs the same type of modification.

A co-owner who makes an exterior modification must maintain liability insurance, underwritten by an insurer authorized to do business in Michigan and naming the association of co-owners as an additional insured, in an amount adequate to compensate for personal injuries caused by the modification. Before a modification is made, the co-owner must submit plans and specifications for the modifications to the association for review and approval.

6.C.12   What are the remedies for violating the Act?

The following are misdemeanors punished by a fine of not more than $10,000 and/or imprisonment for up to one year:

- Willfully misrepresenting the facts as set forth in the recorded master deed
- Knowingly distributing an advertisement pamphlet, prospectus, or letter concerning the project containing a written statement that is false
- Representing a property as a condominium project when it has not been recorded as a condominium project under the terms of this act

Each violation constitutes a separate offense, the terms of imprisonment may run consecutively, and the fines may be aggregated. An action can be brought by the prosecuting attorney of the county in which the property is located, or by the Michigan Department of Attorney General. In addition to any other penalty or remedy, the prosecuting attorney or the attorney general may bring an action to enjoin a violation of the act.

6.C.13   What is the purpose of the Uniform Securities Act, PA 265 of 1964?

The Uniform Securities Act regulates the issuing, offer, sale, and purchase of securities; prohibits fraudulent or misleading practices; and requires the registration of broker-dealers, agents, and investment advisers.

6.C.14   What are securities?

A security is an arrangement in which an investor furnishes capital to an issuer for the operation of an enterprise; and includes the following conditions:

- The capital is at risk.
- A promoter induces the investment by representations that create a reasonable expectation of gain.
- The investor does not intend to be actively involved in the enterprise
- A promoter, at the time the capital is furnished, anticipates that a financial gain may be realized. Examples include notes, stocks, bonds, and other "hands-off" investments.

A *broker-dealer* is a person engaged in the business of buying or selling securities for himself or others. An *agent* is an individual who represents a broker-dealer for the purchase or sale of securities. An *investment advisor* is a person who for a fee advises others, issues analyses or reports concerning securities, or who acts as a finder in conjunction with the offer, sale, or purchase of a security.

6.C.15   Can a real estate licensee sell securities?

Michigan courts have determined that the sale of business stock, including a private sale of a closely held business, is a security. This means that a real estate broker cannot transfer the stock unless he or she is registered as a broker-dealer.

The transfer of the stock of a cooperative apartment, although a security, is usually exempt. The resale of mortgage notes is the sale of a security.

6.C.16   Who may take action and what are the penalties?

The securities administrator may investigate; revoke an exemption; suspend or revoke a registration; issue a cease and desist order; or bring a circuit court action for an injunction or restraining order, accounting or disgorgement, or appointment of a receiver. The administrator may impose a civil fine of up to $1,000 for each violation, not to exceed a total of $10,000.

Also, a person who has been defrauded may bring an action to recover the price paid for the security, plus interest at 6 percent per year, costs, and reasonable attorney fees, minus the amount of income received on the security. Criminal fines are up to $25,000 for each violation and/or imprisonment for up to 10 years.

A complaint must be filed within six years of the offense. However, any time period during which the party was not publicly a resident of Michigan is not included as part of the six years.

D. LANDLORD-TENANT ISSUES

6.D.1   What Michigan law covers landlord-tenant relations?

The Landlord and Tenant Relationship Act, PA 348 of 1972, governs security deposits in Michigan. The Truth in Renting Act, PA 454 of 1978, prevents a landlord from inserting certain types of clauses in a lease agreement.

Anyone who manages even one unit should have a copy of these laws and consult them frequently. The days are gone when the landlord or manager could simply change the locks and toss the tenant's belongings into the street. Today, the tenant has enforceable rights, and if the landlord violates these rights, the landlord may be faced with financial penalties.

6.D.2   Do all leases have to be in writing?

In order to receive legal recognition in the judicial system, the law requires that all lease agreements **over one year** be in writing. Thus, an oral lease for less than a year is enforceable. However, it is important to remember: if it is in writing, you have a prayer; if it's oral, it's just air. It is best to get any lease in writing.

6.D.3   What specific procedures must a landlord follow to evict a tenant?

When a lease has been forfeited, the landlord may use summary proceedings to recover possession. After the time period in a notice to quit has passed, a summons commanding the tenant to appear for trial may be served.

At the trial, the court may issue a judgment for possession. If the tenant does not abide by the judgment willingly, a writ of restitution may then be issued commanding the sheriff to remove the tenant and restore the landlord to possession.

When the eviction is for nonpayment of rent, the writ of restitution will not be issued, if within the time provided, the amount as stated in the judgment, together with the costs, is paid to the landlord. Summary proceedings are in addition to any other remedies available, such as collection of rent. Self-help is never allowed.

6.D.4   What are the requirements for holding and returning a security deposit (i.e., type of account, interest, limits on use, repayment, etc.)?

The security deposit belongs to the tenant and must be placed in a regulated financial institution. The landlord cannot use the money unless he first posts a bond with the secretary of state.

At the termination of the occupancy, the landlord has 30 days to provide the former tenant with an itemized list of damages, including the estimated cost of repair, and a refund of the balance of the deposit. The tenant has seven days to object to the list.

If the tenant objects to the list, the landlord must bring a suit for a money judgment within 45 days of the termination of occupancy, unless the tenant did not leave a forwarding address; did not respond to the list of damages; has entered into a written settlement; or if the entire amount claimed is based on past-due rent. Landlords who violate this provision are subject to double damages.

6.D.5   Can the landlord retain the security deposit?

A security deposit can be used to reimburse for actual damage to the premises, excluding wear and tear. Or the landlord can retain the deposit for past due rent or rent due for premature termination and/or for utility charges.

6.D.6   Is there a maximum amount that a landlord may charge for a security deposit?

A security deposit cannot exceed the equivalent of 1 1/2 month's rent. This includes any prepaid rent other than the amount that is due for the first rental period, or any amount that will be returned to the tenant based on the condition of the rental unit at the end of the term, such as a refundable cleaning fee or pet deposit.

Within 14 days of occupancy, the tenant must receive notice of the landlord's name and address, and a specifically worded statement, in a certain size type, advising the tenant that he or she is required to leave a forwarding address within four days after moving out.

6.D.7   Is an inventory checklist required?

The landlord must provide the tenant with inventory checklists at the beginning of the occupancy. The checklist must contain a specific statement, in a certain size type, advising the tenant that he or she has seven 7 days to record the condition of various items and return the checklist to the landlord. At the end of the occupancy, the landlord will use an identical copy of the checklist to record any damage to the premises.

6.D.8   Where does the landlord go to evict a tenant?

The landlord can go to state district courts, municipal courts, and the common pleas court of Detroit.

6.D.9   What is the Truth in Renting Act?

This act prohibits the insertion of clauses in which the tenant

- waives rights or remedies, including the right to a jury trial;
- releases the landlord of obligations that are imposed by law; or
- violates the consumer protection act or other laws.

A landlord cannot obtain a confession or judgment or a security interest in the tenant's personal property through a clause in the lease. The act also places affirmative duties on the landlord to provide the tenant with his name and address for the purpose of legal notices.

It even requires specific language and certain size of type for a disclosure advising the tenant to seek assistance with the agreement. However, lease agreements in which the clauses are limited to the identity of the parties, description of the premises, rental period, total rent due, amount of rental payments, and the due dates are exempt.

E. OTHER LAWS AFFECTING REAL ESTATE LICENSEES

6.E.1   What is the Michigan Consumer Protection Act, PA 331 of 1976?

This act prohibits those involved in trade or commerce, including real estate brokers and salespersons, from engaging in unfair, unconscionable, or deceptive methods, acts, or practices. A complete list of examples may be found by consulting the act.

A consumer, a prosecuting attorney, or the attorney general may bring a class action for the actual damages caused by an unlawful trade practice. They may also bring an action to obtain a declaratory judgment specifying that a particular practice is unlawful, or to enjoin a person who is engaging in, or is about to engage in, an unlawful trade practice.

A consumer who suffers loss as a result of a violation of this act may bring an action to recover actual and consequential damages or $250, whichever is greater, together with reasonable attorney fees. A consumer's recovery is limited to actual damages if the defendant shows that the violation resulted from a bona fide error in spite of procedures reasonably intended to avoid the error.

An action must be brought within six years of the alleged unlawful practice, or within one year after the last payment in a transaction involving the practice, whichever occurs last.

6.E.2   What Acts cover interest rates and other credit issues?

Multiple acts affect interest rates in Michigan. Real estate licensees should be aware of those acts that set maximum interest rates for loans secured by real estate including PA 326 of 1966 and criminal usury in PA 259 of 1968. Some business entities are exempt from usury statute (PA 52 of 1970 and the Credit Reform Act is PA 162 of 1995).

6.E.3   What activities are regulated?

The maximum interest rate for private parties is 5 percent per annum, except where the agreement is in writing, in which case it is 7 percent per annum. A bank, savings bank, savings and loan association, credit union, or secondary mortgage lender may charge a maximum of 25 percent per annum. A private party issuing a mortgage loan or a land contracts vendor may charge a maximum of 11 percent per annum. A lender that charges more than these maximum rates is engaged in usury.

Criminal usury occurs when a person charges interest on the loan at a rate exceeding 25 percent per annum, or the equivalent rate for a longer or shorter period. Possession of usurious loan records occurs when a person possesses any instrument, with knowledge of its contents, used to record transactions prohibited by this act.

6.E.4   Are there any exceptions?

The maximums only apply to private party consumers and do not apply to interest rates that have been expressly authorized by the Public Service Commission, the Securities Bureau of the Department of Commerce, or where any other law of this state regulates the rate. A corporation, trust, estate, partnership, cooperative, association, or a business may agree to any interest rate charged by a bank, savings bank, savings and loan association, credit union, an insurance carrier, or the finance subsidiary of a manufacturing corporation. This means that the criminal usury rate does not apply to these loans.

In real estate, private parties (noninstitutional lenders) to nonresidential land contract or mortgage loan, with an original secured principal balance of $100,000 or more, may agree to any interest rate. Since criminal usury is 25 percent, the interest rate may not exceed that amount. Processing fees, closing fees, late fees, and NSF fees are not considered interest.

6.E.5　What are the civil and criminal penalties for any violation?

Usury is a defense, which means that a court of law will not enforce an action for collection of any interest that exceeds the legal rate. A borrower that willing pays a noncriminal usurious interest rate will not recover the amount paid, but if a borrower objects, the lender will not be able to collect any interest or charges.

A borrower, a prosecuting attorney, or the attorney general may bring an action to recover $1,000 or actual damages. A lender that willingly and knowingly violates the law may be fined up to $10,000, whereas a lender that persistently violates the act may be fined up to $20,000. Injunctions and class actions are also available.

A person found guilty of criminal usury may be imprisoned up to five years and/or fined up to $10,000. A person found guilty of possession of usurious loan records may be imprisoned for up to one year and/or fined up to $1,000.

6.A.6　What is the State Housing Development Authority Act of 1966, PA 346 of 1966?

The Michigan State Housing Development Authority (MSHDA) provides financial and technical assistance through public and private partnerships in order to create affordable housing for residents of low and moderate income. MSHDA funds public housing projects, provides loans for home improvements and mortgages, and administers various federal housing programs.

MSHDA loans are originated through private, participating lenders. Mortgage funds are allocated on a first-come, first-serve basis, not by lender or by region. MSHDA is funded by the sale of bonds to investors, not through tax revenues. Loans are available for single-family owner occupied homes, including condominiums, co-ops, and manufactured homes. Some programs are also available to landlords and developers.

Loan programs are designed to assist low-income and moderate-income families. To qualify, the borrower's income cannot exceed 115 percent of the greater of statewide median gross income or the area median gross income.

Current income limits are $54,750 in metropolitan counties and $43,575 in other counties. The programs also set purchase price limits.

6.E.7   What types of programs are available?

- *Single family mortgage program*—A low interest rate program for the purchase of owner-occupied, single-family homes.
- *Down payment assistance program*—A zero-interest, deferred-loan program to assist with down payments and closing costs for borrowers who meet more restrictive income qualifications. This program is used in conjunction with MSHDA single-family mortgages or FHA financing.
- *Mortgage credit certificate program (MCC)*—Provides federal income tax credit for part of the interest paid on an owner-occupied, single-family mortgage loan. This is a first-time homebuyer program, that is, the borrower did not own a house in the last three years, and is not refinancing. The IRS considers the MCC a subsidy and may require a recapture of the tax savings if the house is sold during the first nine years.
- *Property improvement program (PIP)*—Low interest rate program for maintenance and improvement of owner-occupied and rental property. The rental program has no income limits for borrowers but the gross rent on each unit cannot exceed MSHDA community rental limits.
- *Multifamily housing development*—Provides loans for the construction, maintenance, and management of housing developments geared to low-income and moderate-income families. A variety of programs are available.

The act contains detailed procedures for judicial foreclosure and foreclosure by advertisement. The law also details the borrower's redemption rights.

6.E.8   What are the Due-on-Sale Clauses, PA 351 of 1984?

A due-on-sale clause is a clause in a mortgage loan that authorizes the lender to declare the loan due and payable if the property is sold or transferred without the lender's prior written consent. Examples include assumption sales and land contracts with underlying loans. The act applies to loans which contain due-on-sale clauses that are secured by residential real estate, that is, 1–4 family dwellings, cooperatives, and residential manufactured homes.

A due-on-sale clause in a mortgage loan originated after October 15, 1982, is fully enforceable. A lender has limited enforcement ability for loans originated during the window period between January 5, 1977, and ending on October 15, 1982.

The act mandates that sales contracts for residential property that will be subject to a mortgage contain a statement specifying that the seller cannot be released from liability under the loan without the lender's consent.

The law applies to state-chartered lenders. The law does not apply to federally chartered lenders; the Garn-St. Germain Depository Institutions Act of 1982 regulates those. For loans originated during the window period, the lender may require that the new borrower qualify, or may offer a blended, or averaged, rate.

6.E.9   What are the remedies if a lender tries to inappropriately enforce a clause?

The attorney general, a prosecuting attorney, or any other person may bring an action for a declaratory judgment that a particular practice violates this act, or an injunction against a lender, real estate broker, or salesperson that is about to engage in a violation. A lender who knowingly attempts to enforce a due-on-sale clause that is in violation of this act may be charged a civil fine of up to $5,000 for each offense.

Any licensee, such as a real estate broker or salesperson, who knowingly advises the seller not to notify a required lender or who assists a seller in evading the law is subject to a civil fine of up to $5,000 and the revocation of his or her license. Anyone who suffers loss as a result of a violation of this act may bring an action to recover actual damages or $250, whichever is greater, plus reasonable attorney fees.

6.E.10   Do mortgage lenders require licensing?

Yes. The Mortgage Brokers, Lenders, and Servicers Licensing Act, PA 173 of 1987, requires that lenders be licensed. A license or registration is required in order for a person to act as a mortgage broker, mortgage lender, or mortgage servicer. The law also prohibits persons from making false statements about loans or their availability.

A mortgage broker is a person who, directly or indirectly, acts as an agent for a person attempting to obtain or make a mortgage loan. A mortgage lender is a person who, directly or indirectly, makes or offers to make mortgage loans. A mortgage servicer is a person who, directly or indirectly, services or offers to service mortgage loans.

6.E.11   Under what circumstances are real estate licensees exempt from registration?

The law applies to real estate brokers and salespersons who fit these definitions, unless they are exempt. This act does not apply to a salesperson acting as an agent for a licensed residential builder. A real estate licensee who acts as a mortgage broker in connection with a real estate sale or lease without additional compensation beyond the customary commission on the sale or lease is exempt.

A real estate licensee who acts as a mortgage broker, lender, or servicer on ten or fewer mortgage loans in a 12-month period from July 1 to June 30 is exempt even if he or she is compensated by the employing real estate broker or receives other additional compensation. Licensees are also exempt if they service only 75 or fewer land contracts, of which ten or fewer require the collection of money for the payment of taxes or insurance.

Real estate licensees must register if they receive additional compensation beyond the customary commission on the real estate sale or lease. A licensee who acts as a mortgage broker, lender, or servicer for property that he or she has not sold or leased must register. Also, a real estate broker must register when the individual licensees may not have met the ten mortgage loan threshold for a mortgage broker, but where the office in aggregate brokered more than 30 mortgage loans.

6.E.12   *What are the civil and/or criminal penalties for violations of not registering?*

The Commissioner of the Office of Financial and Insurance Services of the Department of Consumer and Industry Services may receive complaints, conduct investigations, and issue suspensions. These parties may bring an action for a declaratory judgment that a particular practice violates this act, or an injunction against a person who is about to engage in a violation.

Anyone who suffers loss as a result of a violation of this act may bring an action to recover actual damages, or $250, whichever is greater, plus reasonable attorney fees and costs. A person's recovery is limited to actual damages if the licensee or registrant shows that the violation was not willful, intentional, or the result of gross negligence.

Under Section 18d, any current or former executive officer, director, agent, or control person who violates a final order is guilty of a misdemeanor punishable by a fine of not more than $5,000 and/or imprisonment for up to one year.

Title Issues

Encumbrances can affect the property value, its title marketability, and transferability. This chapter covers basic information about Michigan-specific rules regarding property taxes; encumbrances such as licenses, easements, and adverse possession; and zoning regulations.

A. MICHIGAN PROPERTY TAXES

7.A.1 What is Michigan's fiscal year?

Michigan's fiscal year begins on October 1 of one calendar year and ends on September 30 in the next calendar year. December 31 is property tax day.

7.A.2 How are properties assessed?

Real property taxes are assessed annually, as of tax day, December 31. Michigan property taxes are assessed ad valorem, or according to value. Assessed value cannot exceed 50 percent of the cash value, or market value, of all real property.

A taxpayer must be sent an assessment notice indicating an increase in the tentative equalized valuation or taxable value at least ten days before the meeting of the township Board of Review. The Board of Review meets on the Tuesday immediately following the first Monday in March to review the assessment roll, make adjustments, and certify and approve the roll.

7.A.3 Why do real estate agents need to know about property tax computations?

Proposal A, enacted by the voters of Michigan in 1994, amended the Michigan Constitution to limit annual real estate tax increases. Although the assessed and equalized value of the real estate continues to increase, the annual tax increase is limited to an amount based on the increase in the preceding year's general price level, or 5 percent. Transfer of ownership, however, will "uncap" the tax, and the new owner will be taxed at the correct equalized value.

Agents should acquire basic knowledge about basic property tax assessments and time frames since property taxes can influence asking prices and offered prices. Often, taxes will change when a property has been transferred to new owners, especially those properties that have enjoyed limited increased assessments.

7.A.4 Can a property owner challenge a reassessment?

Yes, a property owner can challenge a reassessment. The owner can attend a second meeting of the Board of Review that is scheduled for the second Monday in March and at least the following Tuesday to hear protests. Some townships or cities require that the property owner first appeal to the assessor prior to protesting to the Board of Review.

If a taxpayer is still unhappy, he or she may appeal to the Michigan tax tribunal. The taxpayer must exhaust all remedies at the Board of Review prior to appearing before the tax tribunal.

The assessment roll must then be delivered to the county equalization director no later than ten days after last meeting, or the first Monday in April.

7.A.5 How are tax rates determined?

Tax rates are reflective of all approved state, county, city, schools, and special budgets. Tax rates also consider all sources of income. After deducting the anticipated ancillary revenue derived from governmental reimbursements, gasoline taxes, fines, sales taxes, motel/hotel taxes, and so on, from the approved budgets, the remainder necessary to cover the costs of the approved budgets is divided by the appropriate taxable value to determine the tax rate.

As previously mentioned in 7.A.3, the Michigan Constitution establishes maximum tax rates and limits annual tax increases.

7.A.6   Is there any possibility of reductions in taxes due?

Tax rates are not usually reduced. Changes occur only when the assessed value decreases, which is rare, or when bond millages expire.

7.A.7   What is Michigan's homestead exemption?

In Michigan, the term *homestead exemption* has a different meaning than it does in other states. In Michigan, the homestead exemption allows the owner to receive a reduction in the amount of school tax that will be assessed.

To qualify as a homestead, an owner must occupy the property as a principal residence and claim a homestead exemption by filing an affidavit on or before May 1 with the local tax assessor's office. If the property is transferred or is no longer the owner's principal residence, the homestead exemption must be rescinded. An owner who fails to rescind an exemption within 90 days of terminating his homestead may be fined a penalty of $5 per day, up to a maximum of $200.

7.A.8   When are property taxes due?

Taxes are due and payable on the date they are billed. Bills are, most often, sent on July 1 and December 1, or on December 1 in communities with one tax date. The amounts assessed become a lien on December 1, or on any other date provided by a city or village charter.

Property tax covers a time period that extends for 12 months, regardless of how many times a year it is paid. Taxes are levied on a calendar year basis, that is, for the calendar year stated. They will be prorated either on a calendar, due-date, or fiscal-year basis. The fiscal year runs in accordance with the fiscal year of the taxing unit and will vary based on the entity. When using the due date, the year begins on the date that the government entity considers the tax due. This can be confusing because the due date that is being referred to is usually the bill or payable date as referenced above, not December 31.

7.A.9   How are the due taxes paid when the property is sold?

When the property owner sells, taxes are divided between the seller and buyer, or apportioned, or **prorated.** Taxes can be prorated in advance or in arrears. Tax prorations can be calculated on a due-date, calendar-year, or fiscal-year basis. There are several methods that are used for prorating taxes. The method used is dictated by the terms of the purchase agreement between the parties.

Care must be used in drafting Michigan contracts, because the terms used in regard to property tax have precise meanings that may be different than their common usage. Michigan law specifies that in an agreement between private parties, unless stated otherwise, the seller is responsible for that portion of the annual taxes levied during the 12 months immediately preceding, but not including, the day title passes. The seller must pay from the levy date or dates to, but not including, the day title passes, and the buyer is responsible for the remainder of the annual taxes. In this section, levy date means the day on which a general property tax becomes due *and* payable. It is also presumed that taxes are paid in advance, from the levy date.

7.A.10   What time frames must be followed?

Property taxes are paid once or twice a year, depending on the local taxing unit. Some communities will allow half of the tax to be paid at one time of year, and the remainder to be paid at another time of year. Or it may be that different taxes may be billed on different dates of the year. Many communities bill city and school taxes in the summer (July 1), but bill the county tax in the winter (December 1). Others bill all of the taxes in the winter.

Thus, it is incumbent on the real estate licensee to be knowledgeable about property tax due dates. As previously mentioned, bringing taxes current can impact a seller's net proceeds.

7.A.11   At what time must the taxes be paid in order to avoid penalties? What is the penalty?

Tax dates may vary based on locale, but most commonly, taxes are billed on July 1 and December 1. The taxpayer is then given a period of time in which to render payment. Regardless, a tax billed in the previous year becomes delinquent on March 1. On June 1, the county treasurer sends a delinquency notice and a second notice is sent on September 1. On November 1, the county treasurer prepares a list of property that is subject to forfeiture the following March 1. On February 1, the county treasurer sends notices of a schedule of fees that will accrue if the tax remains unpaid.

After March 1, the treasurer adds a 4 percent administration fee and 1 percent interest per month to the amount due. Additional fees are added the longer the taxes remain delinquent.

7.A.12   At what point are properties ordered sold at a tax sale?

On March 1 of the second year following the year in which the tax was billed, the property is forfeited. Forfeiture allows a judgment of foreclosure, but the taxpayer retains possession. A foreclosure petition must be filed by June 15 for all forfeited property that has not been redeemed.

The county treasurer of the state must hold a show cause hearing, after which the foreclosure hearing is held by the circuit court. The foreclosure hearing cannot occur prior to 30 days before March 1, that is, January 30 or 31, in the third year after the tax was billed. A foreclosure may be appealed within 21 days, but the full tax must be paid before the appeal is heard.

7.A.13 Does the delinquent taxpayer have any opportunity to "redeem" his property?

The delinquent taxpayer may redeem the property within 21 days after entry of the judgment of foreclosure. Either the taxpayer or a third party, such as a lender, may redeem the property. A third party that redeems can record a lien for the redemption price.

B. ENCUMBRANCES

7.B.1 What are mechanics' liens in Michigan and who may claim them?

A mechanic's lien, referred to as a *construction lien* in Michigan, is a statutory, equitable lien created in favor of contractors, laborers, and materialmen who have performed work or furnished materials in the erection or repair of a building and who have not been paid. The lien must be filed on the parcel of real estate where the materials were used or the labor was performed and must be filed in the county in which the real estate is located.

In order to place a lien, the claimant must have provided a physical improvement to the real estate. Surveys, architectural planning, real estate commissions, and services that have not made a physical alteration do not qualify.

Those who are eligible to file a mechanic's lien include the following:

- *General contractors*—those who contract directly with the homeowner to provide the entire improvement
- *Contractors*—general contractors and others who contract directly with the homeowner
- *Subcontractors*—those who contract with the contractor or other subcontractors to perform part of the improvement
- *Suppliers*—those who contract with the contractor or subcontractor to provide materials and equipment

- *Laborers*—those who contract with the contractor or subcontractor to provide personal labor

7.B.2   What laws protect property owners from such claims?

The Construction Lien Act, PA 497 of 1980, establishes lien rights in persons who have supplied labor or materials to a construction project, but who have not been paid for their work. It establishes a procedure that can be followed for the purpose of placing or foreclosing a lien against real estate.

The Residential Lien Recovery Fund, established under the Construction Lien Act, protects a homeowner who has paid his or her contractor from being foreclosed upon because the contractor failed to pay a subcontractor, supplier, or laborer. It allows the subcontractor, supplier, or laborer to assert his or her claim for payment against the fund, rather than against the homeowner. To be eligible, the individual must have paid into the fund prior to the date of his contract. Claims are limited to $75,000, to be shared proportionally between all of the claimants. The Residential Lien Recovery Fund only applies to a 1-family to 2-family residential structure.

7.B.3   Of what procedures or documents should property owners be aware?

The following documents are designed to facilitate the flow of information regarding the project and the payments made. It is the claimant's responsibility to inform the homeowner that he exists, and it is the homeowner's responsibility to make certain that everyone is properly paid.

The Notice of Commencement is the announcement to the homeowner that work is beginning. The claimant notifies the homeowner that he or she is involved with the project, providing basic information such as a legal description, the names and addresses of the homeowner, designee (person to receive the notices), general contractor, and so on.

Anyone who contributes labor or materials must provide a Notice of Furnishing to the designee and general contractor within 20 days of beginning work. This notifies the parties that a particular person or company has participated and is entitled to payment.

A Sworn Statement is a list made under oath of all persons who have been hired, together with itemized amounts that have been paid or are due. A sworn statement should be obtained from anyone that is demanding payment.

The Waiver of Lien is a release of the right to file a lien. A partial waiver is a promise not to file a lien for the amount paid but does not release rights for the sums that are still outstanding. A conditional waiver is used where arrangements for payment have been made, but the funds have not been delivered. A full, unconditional waiver is used when a claimant has been paid in full.

Finally, the Claim of Lien must be recorded at the county where the property is located within **90 days** of the claimant's last furnishing of labor or materials. The Foreclosure of Lien must be begun within one year of the date of the recorded claim of lien. Where the claim of lien is older than one year, it may be rendered void by recording a certificate from the circuit court stating that foreclosure has not been commenced.

7.B.4   What is a license?

The word *license* has different meanings. In real estate usage, it can mean permission. For example, someone can allow another to go hunting or fishing on his or her property, or to enter the property to pick apples or get water from a spring. A license is a personal privilege and, as such, it is considered to be *revocable permission,* not a right that transfers with ownership.

7.B.5   How may easements be created in Michigan?

Easements in Michigan can be created expressly by a deed or other conveyance, or by use. Easements are often created by mutual agreement, such as maintenance easements that benefit a homeowner association.

A property owner may acquire a prescriptive easement by using someone else's property adversely, openly (visibly), notoriously, and without permission for a continuous statutory period of 15 years. Tacking is used to determine the time frame that has passed, and one owner is not required to have used the easement for the entire 15-year period.

7.B.6   What time frame must be observed for adverse possession (leading to ownership)?

In order to claim title to ownership in real estate by adverse possession, a person must show that he or she has used the real estate openly, notoriously, continuously, with intent to deprive, and without permission for a period of, generally, 15 years. Some types of claims may be made in shorter time periods. For example, if the possessor obtained a fiduciary deed, the period is only five years.

Tacking is permitted. To prevent adverse possession, the owner can serve written notice to anyone using the land in question that the owner intends to dispute any right arising from such claim or use. Adverse possession is strictly construed and every presumption is made in favor of the original owner. Adverse possession cannot be claimed against the State of Michigan.

7.B.7   What is acquiescence?

Acquiescence is often perceived as adverse possession for property boundaries but is legally quite different. Adverse possession is hostile, but acquiescence involves agreement. Acquiescence can occur where the parties have peaceably used a boundary for the statutory period (generally 15 years); or following a boundary dispute and agreement; or from an intention to convey to a marked boundary.

C.   ZONING ISSUES

7.C.1   Who or what regulates construction?

Members of the National Association of Homebuilders build according to the International Residential Code (IRC), which replaces the latest 1997 edition of the Uniform Building Code (UBC). In addition, the International Building Code is the standard used for commercial building practices in the United States. All builders use standards established by the International Plumbing Code (IPC) as well as the energy code known as CABO.

Michigan is a home rule state, which means that while building officials and builders agree to build according to IRC standards, local building officials and builders (when applicable) can deviate somewhat and adopt alternative standards allowed under the UBC.

7.C.2   Any special zoning terms?

Special zoning called a *planned unit development (PUD)* is used in Michigan to allow for diverse land uses (residential, commercial, recreational) to exist under one umbrella. Converted-use properties need zoning approval. An example is the conversion of warehouses in downtown areas to loft apartments.

7.C.3   What is the source of zoning authority enjoyed by Michigan communities?

Michigan is a home rule state, meaning that local jurisdictions, such as cities and townships, can engage in some degree of self-government. The State of Michigan gives the authority to each local jurisdiction to develop its own zoning regulations for the purpose of promoting the health, safety, morals, or the general welfare of the community. This results in each local jurisdiction having its own land-use regulation, enforced by its local zoning authority, that is, planning commission and boards of zoning appeals.

Zoning provides local communities with the authority to regulate and restrict development. Michigan uses three slightly different enabling acts: the county zoning enabling act, the township zoning enabling act, and the village enabling act.

7.C.4   What are the various types of proper and improper zoning?

Land uses in a zoning ordinance can be ranked from most restrictive (detached single family residential) to least restrictive (heavy industrial). Michigan ordinances can either be cumulative or noncumulative. A *cumulative* ordinance will permit a certain use in a district, as well as any other use that is more restrictive. For example, an area zoned heavy industrial will allow any use, but an area zoned detached single-family resident would only allow that one restrictive use. A *noncumulative* ordinance restricts an area to a particular, single use.

Exclusionary zoning occurs where a particular land use is totally excluded from the municipality. This is unconstitutional discrimination in violation of equal protection. A spot zone, although not per se illegal, will be carefully scrutinized, since it creates a pocket that is inconsistent with the larger zone. Zoning must result in a logical plan that promotes public health, safety, and welfare.

A *nonconforming use* occurs when an area is rezoned so as to make a prior conforming use improper. The property that no longer conforms will be grandfathered, so that it can continue to be used as it was used in the past.

7.C.5   Under what conditions may a developer subdivide?

Zoning is one method that local jurisdictions use to ensure harmonious growth with community standards. However, land developers must also conform to the municipality's subdivision and land development regulations. The land must be surveyed and laid out so that the subdivision utilizes natural drainage and land contours. Often an environmental impact report is required with the application for subdivision approval. Plats have to be adopted by the municipality before they can be recorded.

From the subdivision plans, plats are drawn of the land. The plat divides the land into lots. The plat is then submitted to the municipality for adoption. Often, the developer pays the costs for the streets and sewers, and then the streets and sewers are *dedicated* back to the municipality for its ownership and future maintenance.

D. LAND DIVISION ACT

7.D.1   What state law regulates land division?

The Land Division Act, PA 288 of 1967, regulates the division of land and its orderly layout. The act requires that the area be suitable for building sites and public improvements with adequate drainage, that it is surveyed and conveyed by accurate legal descriptions, and that adequate streets or roads are developed.

The law provides for lot splits that are exempt from approval, defines allowable divisions that require municipal approval, and mandates that subdivisions be platted. Municipal approval is not required for splits that will create parcels of at least 40 acres that are accessible to a road by a driveway or easement.

For more detailed information, consult MCLA 560.109(2), MSA 26.430 and following.

7.D.2   What size are allowable divisions?

Allowable divisions that create at least one parcel 40 acres in size or smaller require municipal approval. The number of parcels that can be created is limited. Two of the most important requirements for obtaining an approval are that (1) each parcel must be accessible to a road, and (2) the depth of a parcel cannot exceed four times its width.

7.D.3   Is there any limitation on the number of parcels in a division?

Yes. The number of parcels allowed in a division depends on the size of the parent parcel or parent tract (original parcel). A property of 10 acres or less can be divided into four parcels. A property of 10 to 120 acres is allowed one additional parcel for every 10 acres, after the first 10 acres. If the parcel is more than 120 acres, another parcel may be added for every 40 acres in the original parent property.

7.D.4   What are bonus parcels?

The law creates incentives for better land use by offering additional splits for large parcels or those that do not directly burden an existing road. A parent parcel of at least 20 acres may receive up to two additional splits if: (1) 60 percent of the original parcel remains intact, or (2) a new road, either public or private, is created, so that no new driveways access the existing road.

7.D.5   Can a property ever be resubdivided?

Once the maximum division has occurred, a redivision cannot occur for another 10 years. If the maximum division has not occurred, the right to additional allowable divisions may be transferred to a new parcel or may remain with the parent parcel.

7.D.6   What is a subdivision?

A subdivision is the splitting of land into parcels that exceed the requirements for an exempt split or an allowable division. A subdivision of land requires the approval of plats by various county agencies (such as the Drain Commissioner, Road Commission, Plat Board) and state agencies (such as the Department of Transportation, Department of Consumer and Industry Services, and Department of Environmental Quality).

7.D.7   What special language must the deed contain when a property is split or subdivided?

A deed conveying an unplatted parcel must contain a statement as to whether the right to make additional allowable divisions is also being conveyed with the parcel. The statement shall be in substantially the following form: "The grantor grants to the grantee the right to make [insert number] division(s) under section 108 of the Land Division Act, Act No. 288 of the Public Acts of 1967." If no statement is made, then the right to make divisions stays with the remainder of the parent tract or parcel that is retained by the grantor.

All deeds for parcels of unplatted land must also contain the following statement: "This property may be located within the vicinity of farm land or a farm operation. Generally accepted agricultural and management practices which may generate noise, dust, odors, and other associated conditions may be used and are protected by the Michigan right to farm act."

7.D.8   What about the disclosure of private roads?

When a parcel, whether platted or unplatted, is serviced by a private road, the purchaser must be notified that the county road commission is not required to maintain the road. The notice must be on a separate instrument attached to the document conveying the parcel.

7.D.9   Can property in a flood plain be developed?

No, a residential building cannot be built within a flood plain shown on a plat.

7.D.10   What are the civil and criminal remedies for dividing law illegally?

The attorney general, a prosecuting attorney, a municipality, board of county road commissioners, or county plat board may bring an action to restrain or prevent any violation of this act or any continuance of a violation. Any sale of lands subdivided or split in violation of this act is voidable at the option of the purchaser. The seller will forfeit all of the consideration received and will be liable for any damages sustained by the purchaser.

Any person who splits land in violation of the allowable division or exempt split provisions, and who sells a resulting parcel of land is responsible for the payment of a civil fine of up to $1,000 for each parcel sold. If the land was required to be platted, agreeing to sell a parcel before the plat is recorded is a misdemeanor punishable by a fine of up to $1,000, and/or imprisonment up to 180 days. For the second and each subsequent offense, the penalty is a fine of up to $1,000 and/or imprisonment for up to one year.

E. OCCUPATIONAL CODE: OUT-OF-STATE LAND SALES

7.E.1   What regulates out-of-state properties if marketed by a Michigan broker?

Sales of out-of-state properties are regulated by Occupational Code, Section 2511(2), and Rules 501- 529.

Real estate brokers who propose to engage in sales of a promotional nature of property located outside of Michigan must receive prior approval from the state of Michigan, through the Department of Consumer and Industry Services. Promotional nature means 25 or more units or lots, whether improved or vacant, including timeshares and right-to-use agreements. The units do not need to be adjacent or contiguous to one another.

A broker who desires to sell out-of state property by advertising in Michigan must be licensed in Michigan. The Michigan broker must submit an application, along with the investigation fee, to the Department. The application must include a submittal of particulars and copies of all proposed documents to be signed by the buyer. The application must also include a copy of the conveyance document, price list, and proposed property report.

7.E.2 Are there any other filing requirements?

When the Michigan Land Sales Act requires registration of the out-of-state property, a copy of the order of registration must be included with the application. If the out-of-state property is exempt from the Michigan Land Sales Act, the broker must submit a copy of his current filing with the office of interstate land sales registration together with his application.

7.E.3 Who is responsible for paying for investigating the property?

The Michigan broker must pay the cost of the Department's investigation of the property. This includes a $500 fee paid at the time of application and the estimated expenses for an on-site inspection, if necessary. However, the broker cannot refer to the investigation by later making claims that the property has been investigated, inspected, or approved for sale by the state of Michigan.

7.E.4 What is meant by full particulars?

The broker must submit full particulars of the property, on a form provided by the Department, containing a full description of the property and the proposed terms of sale. Full particulars must include the following:

- The names and addresses of the broker and the seller
- A general description including the number of units
- Significant terms of any encumbrances, easements, restrictions, zoning, taxes, and assessments
- A statement of use
- Information regarding existing and proposed improvements, including streets; water supply; drainage control; irrigation; sewage disposal; utilities; and the estimated cost, completion date, and responsibility for construction and maintenance
- A description of the promotional plan, together with all advertising materials
- A legal description, a statement of topography, and a map showing the unit dimensions and relation to streets and off-site improvements, together with a statement of the present condition of access, availability of sewage disposal and other public utilities, and distance (in miles) to nearby municipalities

- The nature of the improvements to be installed, along with statements as who will install, who will pay, a schedule of completion, and provisions for maintenance
- Any other information required in order to provide full and fair disclosure

When the out-of-state promotion is for condominiums that are exempt under the Michigan Land Sales Act, the Department may accept a copy of the filing and order from the situs state in fulfillment of the requirements for the submittal of particulars. Similarly, the Department may accept a copy of the filing and order from the situs state in satisfaction of the requirements for the submittal of particulars, for the sale of timeshare or membership interests, when all of the sales are to be conducted in the situs state.

7.E.5   *What is the property report?*

The buyer must receive a property report describing the physical characteristics of the property and any unusual or material aspects of the property. A broker must submit a copy of the proposed property report to the Department on the required forms. Any material change in the information contained in the property report must be immediately reported to the Department, even if the order of approval has already been issued.

7.E.6   *How soon is the order for approval issued and for how long is it valid?*

Upon a broker's compliance with the Department's provisions, an order of approval will be issued allowing a broker to engage in promotional sales. The order is effective for one year from the date of issue and may be renewed annually. The broker must pay the costs of investigation at the time of renewal.

F. LAND SALES ACT

7.F.1   *What is the Land Sales Act, PA 286 of 1972?*

The Land Sales Act applies to the promotional sale of land, whether the land is located inside or outside of Michigan. The out-of-state land sales law and rules and the Michigan Land Sales Act overlap. However, the Michigan Land Sales Act only applies to vacant land, whereas the Occupational Code and the rules apply to any type of interest that is located outside of Michigan but is being promoted in Michigan.

7.F.2   What land must be registered?

Any disposition, that is, sale, lease, option, award, or assignment of lots, parcels, units, or interests in land from subdivisions, requires prior registration. The law also prohibits deceptive trade practices, provides for filing of bonds, and regulates advertisement.

7.F.3   How is subdivision defined under the Land Sales Act?

A subdivision is any land, wherever located, improved or unimproved, consisting of 25 or more lots, parcels, units, or interests. Subdivided lands include land located outside of Michigan if the sale is promoted by mail, telephone calls, solicitation, or advertisements directed into Michigan. The lots are considered part of a subdivision if they are marketed by a common promotional plan of advertising, whether or not they are contiguous, and even if different developers are offering them.

7.F.4   What does the Land Sales Act require?

When subdivision registration is required, the developer may not sell any lots prior to registration. The developer must deliver a current property report to the buyer who must be given time to review it. The developer cannot engage in unfair or deceptive trade practices.

A buyer may cancel any contract if the buyer did not receive a property report prior to the execution of a contract. Or, a buyer may unconditionally rescind any agreement with the developer or revoke any offer within five days from the actual receipt of a legible copy of the signed agreement and the property report.

Each agreement must be prominently labeled as a document taken in connection with the Land Sales Act. Each agreement must prominently contain a notice on its face, in a specified size type, advising the buyer that he or she may cancel the agreement as specified. The notice must provide sufficient space for the buyer's signature acknowledging that he or she has read the notice. A buyer cannot waive the right to rescind.

7.F.5   Are any properties exempt from registration or supervision?

Yes. This law does not apply to dispositions of land by a buyer of subdivided land for his or her own account in a single or isolated transaction or to a builder constructing residential, commercial, or industrial buildings for the purpose of resale or for his or her own use. These exemptions are quite broad and only leave vacant land.

The law does not apply if fewer than 25 separate lots, parcels, units, or interests are offered. Likewise, a parcel is exempt if there is a commercial or industrial building, shopping center, or dwelling unit (that is, house, condo, co-op, or apartment), or where the seller has a legal obligation to construct such a building within two years from date of disposition.

The act does not apply to buying cemetery lots, a parcel pursuant to a court order, or registered or exempted securities. It does not apply to a subdivision that has a plan of sale to dispose to ten or fewer persons, or to a person electing to make dispositions under any two or more different exemptions, or to a campground or a mobile home park developed according to Michigan law. It does not apply to a subdivision that has fewer than 50 lots, parcels, units, or interests, and that has been fully recorded under the Land Division Act, or to the owner of adjacent land on which there is a commercial or industrial building, shopping center, dwelling unit, or apartment. Finally, it does not apply to land that is used or will be used for agricultural purposes.

7.F.6   *What must the property report contain?*

A property report must be provided to a buyer and filed with the Department. The property report cannot be used for promotional purposes or to imply that the property has been investigated or approved by the State of Michigan.

The property report must fully and accurately disclose the physical characteristics of the subdivided lands offered and must make known to prospective buyers all unusual and material conditions relating to noise, health, safety, and welfare that affect the subdivision and are known to the developer. The proposed property report submitted to the department must essentially contain the same information as required for a submission of particulars for out-of-state land sales under the Occupational Code. Plus, as required by the Land Division Act, the report must also contain the notice that the property may be in the vicinity of a farm operation.

7.F.7   *Can a developer use blanket encumbrances?*

A developer cannot sell lots in a subdivision that are subject to a blanket encumbrance, such as a blanket mortgage, unless he or she provides for the buyers' protection in one of the following ways:

- Paying all funds into escrow
- Placing the fee title in trust until each encumbrance is released
- Posting a bond
- Subordinating the blanket encumbrance

7.F.8   What civil penalties may be imposed on violators?

The attorney general can bring an action in an amount equal to treble (3 times) the unpaid fees when a developer who has not paid the required fees continues to sell lots.

The Department may issue cease and desist orders, require a person to perform affirmative acts, revoke a registration, issue injunctive relief or a temporary restraining order, appoint a receiver or conservator, or require a bond. Every owner or person in control of a development company, or any employee or agent, who materially aids in the disposition is also liable jointly and severally and to the same extent as the developer.

A developer is liable to a buyer for: (1) disposing of subdivided lands without registration; (2) failure to provide a property report; (3) engaging in a deceptive practice; or (4) making an untrue statement of a material fact or omitting a material fact that is required to be stated. The buyer may recover the price paid for the lot, together with interest at the rate of 6 percent per year from the date of payment, plus any property taxes paid, costs and reasonable attorneys' fees, minus profit realized at the time of reconveyance.

7.F.9   Are there any criminal penalties?

Yes, it is a felony to knowingly make a false statement or misrepresentation and to knowingly fail to comply with the terms of a final cease and desist order. It is also a felony to distribute an advertisement, pamphlet, prospectus, or letter with knowledge that it contains a false statement.

Each developer or agent may be fined up to $25,000 and/or imprisoned for up to 10 years. Each violation constitutes a separate offense. Any violation of this act, other than as stated above, is a misdemeanor and subject to a fine of up to $2,000 and/or imprisonment for up to 90 days for each offense.

7.F.10   What is the statute of limitations under the Land Sales Act?

An action must be brought within three years from the time of performance of all representations contained in any registration statement, property report, purchase agreement, contract, option, or other document, but not more than six years after the sale or lease to the buyer.

Where the cause of action arises out of a deceptive practice or the omission of a material fact, the action must be brought within three years of the date the buyer discovers deceit or omission.

G. RIGHT TO FARM ACT

7.G.1   *What is the purpose of the Michigan Right to Farm Act?*

This law facilitates agriculture, Michigan's second leading industry and its second largest employer. Persons moving into a farming community may not bring suit for the odors, dust, and noise that farm operations produce.

The Michigan Right to Farm Act, PA 93 of 1981, allows farmers to defend themselves from nuisance suits by showing that they follow established agricultural practices. The law applies to all farm operations for crops and food production, marketing produce, operating machinery, ground and aerial seeding and spraying, application of fertilizers, liming material and pesticides, care of animals, storage, utilization, and application of farm waste.

7.G.2   *What farming operations are permitted?*

A farm operation is not considered a public or private nuisance if the operation conforms to generally accepted agricultural and management practices. It is also not a nuisance if the farm existed before a change in the land use, or occupancy of land, within one mile of the boundaries of the farm, and if before that change in use, the farm would not have been a nuisance.

A farm operation that is in conformance with generally accepted agricultural and management practices is not a public or private nuisance as a result of a change in ownership or size or temporary cessation or interruption of farming. Farmers do not lose their rights by enrolling in governmental programs, adopting new technology, or changing the type of farm product being produced.

7.G.3   *How are complaints investigated?*

The Michigan Department of Agriculture investigates all complaints involving a farm operation, such as complaints involving the use of manure and other nutrients; agricultural waste products; dust, noise, odor, fumes, air pollution, surface water, or groundwater pollution; food and agricultural processing by-products; care of farm animals; and pest infestations.

If it is determined that the problem was caused by the use of other than generally accepted agricultural and management practices, the farm will be advised that changes should be made to resolve the problem and to conform with generally accepted practices. The farm may be required to file an implementation plan.

7.G.4   Are there any penalties for repeated, unfounded complaints?

A complainant who brings more than three unverified complaints against the same farm within three years may be ordered to pay the Department the full costs of its investigation for the fourth or any subsequent unverified complaint against the same farm.

In any nuisance action brought against a farm operation where the farm prevails, the farm may recover from the plaintiff its actual amount of costs and expenses of defense, together with actual attorney fees.